He is a retired p[illegible]parative literature, originally from Ira[illegible] Arab universities until in 2004, he was invit[illegible]heikh Mohammed bin Rashid Al Maktoum of Dubai, [illegible] be his cultural adviser. In July 2012, he started his 'active retirement' and settled in Cambridge, UK, producing seven books of critical studies and translations Arabic/English/Arabic. His published works have reached fifty-seven.

Dedication

To the memory of a genuine modern Iraqi poet.

Abdulrazzaq Abdulwahid

MODERN IRAQI POETRY

A POET FOR ALL SEASONS

AUSTIN MACAULEY PUBLISHERS™
LONDON • CAMBRIDGE • NEW YORK • SHARJAH

A CIP catalogue record for this title is available from the British Library.

ISBN 9781788483933 (Paperback)
ISBN 9781788483940 (Hardback)
ISBN 9781788483957 (E-Book)

www.austinmacauley.com

First Published (2018)
Austin Macauley Publishers Ltd™
25 Canada Square
Canary Wharf
London
E14 5LQ

Preface

I met Abdulrazzāq Abdulwāḥid for the first time in my first year at the École Normale Supérieure in Baghdad, in1948. He was in the Department of Arabic, and I was in the Department of Foreign Languages. My love of poetry soon made me a close friend of this prize-winning poet, in all the 10 am public sessions of every Thursday at the École. We remained close friends, and kept contact by phone and email, especially in our years of diaspora, from the early 1980s, until his departure in a Paris hospital on 8th Novemeber, 2015.

Judging by this close knowledge of the poet, I can say that he was a genuine Iraqi, not related to any political creed or party. Before the 2003 American invasion of Iraq, no one cared whether the person sitting next to you was of this or that religion, or political persuasion. You could probably tell whether that man or woman was a Muslim or Christian, of this religious sect or the other, when you heard the name of that person. Many names were common to both Muslims and Christians. In my school days, there was a pupil in our class from a wealthy Christian family whose name was Hāshim, the name of the grandfather of Prophet Moḥammad. I never knew, or ever asked Abdulrazzāq about his religion, or sect. But in 1986, I was invited to a poetry festival in Riaḍ, Saudi Arabia. We were a group of Iraqis, waiting for the arrival of Abdulrazzāq who was in Cairo, for a memorial of the two major Egyptian poets: Shawqi and Ḥāfiẓ. When he finally arrived, he came with a big smile on his face, and started telling us, sarcastically, that he was delayed and questioned at Riaḍ airport about his 'religion' which took the authorities two hours to understand what 'sabean' meant, whether it was a religion, and why was he not a Muslim, since he was Iraqi! This was the first time I knew, from the poet, that he belonged to that peaceful and friendly minority in Amara, in the water blessed south of Iraq.

Yet, there is not a single reference to that religious persuasion in the entire corpus of the poet. Similarly, there is not a single reference to any political or religious party in the more than fourty collections of poetry by this unique and genuine Iraqi poet, published from 1950 to shortly before his demise in 2015.

It is regrettably common that the outstanding talent has no shortage of envious, non-talented, semi-educated literally parasites around him. Some of these were contaminated by the pseudo-political persuasions, and seasonal gusts of hero worship, only to prove that they were readymade turncoats. Such outsiders coined the title of 'The Poet Laureate of Ṣaddām regime', to describe the poet ‹Abdulrazzāq ‹Abdulwāḥid.

The fact is that our poet had an admiration for the 'character' of Ṣaddām, not for his politics, which may be difficult to swallow by the 'politico paths'. The war against Iran in 1980-8 was justified by millions of Iraqis, though not so was the invasion of Kuwait in 1991. Of these million Iraqis was the poet ‹Abdulrazzāq, and he was quite vocal about it; lately on television too. A political conviction, like a religious conviction, cannot be argued, or, indeed, compromised, on a moral or personal level. In the case of the poet or the artist as a whole, the product should be evaluated on its own merit.

A whole decade has passed over the end of Ṣaddām and his regime. A nonbiased look at 'Shī ‹ite' and 'Iranianite' Iraq has seen a gradual, new revaluation of Ṣaddām's attitude towards Iran, and of the unfair accusation that Ṣaddām was against the Iraqi Shī ‹ites. A review of the cabinets and the army under Ṣaddām shows no such bias against Shī ‹ite, Christian or any ethnic minorities. In fact, very recently, an Iraqi Shī ‹ite cleric was wondering, in the very significant

Friday prayers sermon, whether it was not time to apologise to Ṣaddām about his unfair accusation of mistreatment of Iraqi Shī ‘ites. It takes courage and immunity against danger to express an attitude secretly held by the majority of modern day Iraqis, who can see, with two eyes, what is happening in Iraq. Some courageous souls remember the last words Ṣaddām uttered on the gibbet, when one of his prosecutors shouted, “Now you go to hell!” Ṣaddām was very cool and answered, “After me, Iraq will be hell.”

One example of the poet’s admiration of Ṣaddām’s character was shown lately on a TV video. This was an interview with the poet which Ṣaddām wanted. The poet was answering questions about poetry and other cultural matters in a very intimate session. The poet felt like smoking, and asked Ṣaddām permission to do so. Ṣaddām readily offered the poet one of his exquisite Havana cigars, which the poet politely declined, reaching for his own brand of cigarettes. But the poet was stunned to see Ṣaddām go down on his knees, with a matchbox to light the poet’s cigarette. Utterly embarrassed, the poet tried to take the matchbox from Ṣaddām’s hands, saying “Impossible!” Ṣaddām, still on his knees, retorted, “Why impossible? Are you not Arabian?” The poet, shivering, answered, “Arabian, yes, but not that far!”

This may be hard, very hard, to believe, if one only heard this about the interview, without seeing the video. But this is one example to explain the poet’s admiration of Ṣaddām, outside the political aura. Is that possible?

In recent years, some Arabic TV programmes tried to embarrass ‘Abdulrazzāq about his admiration of the ‘otherwise dictator’, writing poems in his honour, and praising his courage. Now that Ṣaddām was gone, can the poet speak out his mind and say why he admired a ‘dictator’. The answer was always, “I was not praising the president in him, but the symbol he represents of Iraq and the homeland”. Again, can you honestly argue a man out of his convictions?

As a genuine poet, ‘Abdulrazzāq was an Iraqi Arab in all the poetry he wrote. He sang of Arab Iraq and of the Arab nation as a whole in the various countries, especially about Palestine. And, as a genuine Iraqi Arab poet, he wrote heart touching poems about the Shī ‘ite eminent figures: Ali, Al-Ḥusain, and the Shī ‘ite holy places. His unique dramatic poem about the martyrdom of Al-Ḥusain could lead the naive reader to think the poet was Shī ‘ite. But the head-in-the-sand envious ‘poetasters’ and the politically sham critics have never stopped howling at the moon. In the wake of the poet’s departure, one self-installed critic in the so called ‘Writers Union’ could not find enough morality in himself to say a few kind words about a departed eminent poet of his ‘own country’. Accusing the poet of being a ‘Ba‘thist’, he brought the ‘proof’ to his claim in reading that beautifully painful poem, ‘Do not knock on the door’ as expression of ‘sorrow for the departure of the Ba‘th party and Ṣaddām followers’. Had that ‘clever’ critic only read the poem he would have found that it was the grief of a father who came home in the evening and knocked at the door, expecting his children to come and open for him, as they used to do when they were small children. Now that they have grown up, and, like thousands of Iraqi young men and women, have left to other lands looking for work, but mainly to escape danger in collapsing Iraq. The poet, momentarily deranged, could not realise they have departed, so he had to use his own keys to enter a house without his children, no longer a ‘home’.

*****

The poems I present in this volume were culled from over forty collections published in the poet’s lifetime. I have reluctantly avoided the many beautiful and very significant poems written in the traditional meter and the two hemistiches style. This is partly because the beauty in those poems is informed by the rhetorical devices, the tone of the rhyme, and several other linguistic qualities of Arabic, which are next to impossible to render in any other language, let alone English. The use of the dual in nouns, pronouns, adjectives and verbs cannot be represented in a language which does not recognise the dual. The allusions to historical events and prominent figures in the Arab history, used in those traditional style poems, cannot be done justice in footnotes. The poems I thought would give a true image of the poetic talent were the majority written in the 'metric style' where the 'foot' rather than the two hemistiches style conveys the idea or the image better, irrespective of the number of feet in the traditional Arabic prosody. This style was significantly initiated by the pioneer poet Nāzik Al-Malā'ika (1923–2007) though she gave it the misnomer of free verse.

My selections come in four sections: Of the Homeland, Of Love, Of Other Concerns, and a Dramatic Poem. The first section is a true mirror of the poet's love of Iraq and the Arab nation. The history of ancient Iraq and civilisation are emphasised. The foreign designs, political and religious against the Arabs, act as a background to more recent foreign designs against Iraq and the Arab Islamic nations, portrayed in the failed attempt of the Ethiopian Christian governor, Abraha, against ancient Arabia, in 'The Year of the Elephant'. The aggression against the Arab Palestinians in Ṣabra, Shateela, and Tal-al- Zaʿtar in modern Lebanon are yet another example of the ongoing aggression against the Palestinian Arabs.

The second section, 'On Love', is a pleasant fresh breeze of human feelings, when love is brought down to earth in the language of the day. Yet it is free from the sentimentality of the French *fin de siècle* quality which was the hallmark of much of the love poetry of a couple of decades earlier.

The third section, 'Of Other Concerns', presents the poet as a human being of this time and age, conscious of his national culture, historical and religious. He speaks to us of feelings and emotions familiar to us all, and reminds us of our historical and cultural background, with the references which we should keep close to our hearts.

The fourth and last section is a unique Dramatic Poem in three acts, unjustly called by the poet 'a play in three acts';

but it is a full-fledged drama in the Aristotelian sense. It is the tragedy of the fall of Al-Ḥusain ibn ʿAli, in an intricate foul play of politics and religiosity. The son of the last Muslim Caliph was led, or rather misled, by a section of Muslim ʿArabs who were viciously manipulated by those who usurped power, using their army as 'hunting dogs', only to lead their army generals to a very late realization of their predicament, a *peripeteia* in the Aristotelian dramatic sense, where the only solution was their suicide.

Cambridge, June 2016 Abdulwāḥid Lu'lu'a

Biographical Notes

*The poet was born in Baghdad, Iraq, in 1930. His family moved back to their hometown of ‹Amara in the south of Iraq, where he spent part of his childhood and early years; then he returned with the family to the capital Baghdad where he completed his schooling and joined the École Normale Supèrieure, the only university institution where languages and humanities were taught, before the establishment of the Faculty of Arts in the early 1950s. In the École the major Iraqi poets graduated, and that is where the young man thrived as a poet, graduating with honours in 1952.

*He taught Arabic at schools until 1970, when he was moved to the Ministry of Culture, where he became editor-in-chief of a major literary monthly; then he was appointed Director of the Musical Studies Institute, then a Dean of the Arab Documents Institute.

*In 1987, he was promoted to a special cultural advisor, and director general of the National Library.

*He published more than forty-five collections of poetry, ten of which are poetry for children, of which he was very proud.

*Among the many honours and prizes, he was awarded:

- The Pushkin Medal, International Poetry Festival, Moscow 1976.
- The Cambridge Coat of Arms and the Order of Merit, 1979.
- The Golden Poem Medal, International Poetry Festival, Macedonia 1986.
- The State Medal for Literature, Baghdad 1987.

- The First Prize, International Poetry Festival, Belgrade, 1990.

*He left one daughter and three sons, eight grandchildren of boys and girls.

*****

Of the Homeland

*****

Genesis

When it was rounded
When all its signs were formed,
The sun was ordered to keep a site, and not leave,
The star was ordered to keep nearby.
Then turns were marked on the Earth,
Where water sprang in between,
And two signs withdrew,
Flowing, by a miracle.
Then met the dawn with the night,
The fire with the water,
Each by order, driven.
And came the voice,
Be…
And Iraq was!
Dawn of all life,
Cradle of all prophets,
Since the time of Adam,
And of civilizations, since the time of Ur; (1)
The start of all ages,
Since the birth of Sumer. (2)
Round it all suns turn.

Babylon sun shone,
Then Akkad light followed. (3)

After them came Ashur, (4)
In whose hands were left
The reins of power;
Then destiny turned to sleep.
On waking,
The star of Iraq
Was shining in Hatra! (5)

Then came Baghdad,
Carrying the candles of A Thousand and One Nights,
With the voice of Scheherazade,
And the finest dreams about Sinbad sails.
She raised Al-Rasheed,
And enjoyed a thousand new dawns,
After which long darkness prevailed,
Until in her night twinkled
A star, coming on a day of feast.
Who knows Iraq?
Who knows how plains and mountains meet,
Light and shades,
Reality and imagination,
The possible, and impossible?

Who knows Iraq?
The haven of Noah's Ark,
In his great Flood;
The house of Ibraheem,
Where he raised his light;
And the ascent of Shāmash (6)
The voice of Gilgamesh, (7)
The steps of the Ziqqurāt, (8)
The impregnable cachets;
The water running up, supernaturally,
To the Hanging Gardens.

Who knows Iraq?
Who knows what destiny lies

In this land, where destiny decreed
That in her loin's heaven and hell should meet.

Here is Iraq.
Not once was it besieged
But a giant from its sleep awoke,
Roaring, so the seven heavens called for help,
At the sight of its gushing blood.

This is Iraq,
Lately, when men bent their heads,
And the headband was about to cry,
Iraq's head remained like mountain tops.

The war raged,
Infants, children and the elderly were massacred;
But Iraqi pinnacles remained high.

Iraq is the descendant of glory and honor
The Homeland, where everyone is a prophet's grandchild.
As if the entire grandeur of the entire earth,
Belongs to it; there everyone is my father.
This is Iraq, so tell misfortunes to cease,
The entire time turned old, but Iraq is still young.

Notes:

1. Ur: the Sumerian city-state, traditionally the home of Ibrahim, before he left to the land of Kanaan. It was inhabited until about 450 BC.
2. Sumer: The first civilisation in the world. Established the cuneiform script, about 3000 BC, as the first script known to humanity.
3. Akkad: The earliest kingdom in the south of Mesopotamia, in the old bronze age of 3000 BC.
4. Ashur: The earliest empire in Mesopotamia in the third millennium BC.
5. Hatra: First Arabian kingdom in northern Mesopotamia. It withstood the Roman invasion in 116 and 198 A.D. It had a flourishing great civilisation.
6. Shamash: The god of sun and justice, from whom Hammurabi received the first laws known to humanity.
7. Gilgamesh: The first great work of literature known in the world, coming from Mesopotamia in the third millennium BC.
8. Ziqqurat: Late third millennium BC buildings for worship in ancient Mesopotamia: Sumer, Babylon, Ashur, and Akkad.

Year of the Elephant

The plate reads:
    The Sun darkens for seven days
    The Earth burns for seven days
        And they mix.
Then they burn together,
    Then they darken,
        And smoke prevails.

Between a murdered night and a murdered mid-morning,
The Year of the Elephant begins. (1)

Here they are,
    All mornings will spread wings,
        Which give no light.
The nights will call in their calm,
But their calm does not come.

Who saw Abraha?
    I saw him.
I saw blood shedding from his mouth corners,
Down, to his neck.
He was writhing as if stung,
    Beating his head,
        With his hands and fangs,
Beating on the Iraqi sand-barrier.

One night I said to him,
    You are mistaken,

Your grandfather did not come from about
Baghdad.
He said, the ends are the same.
He meant to reach the Home of Hope.
The road to it
Begins from Karbalā'. (2)

Who saw Abraha?

He was not simply an army with elephants,
It was a sign of evil times.
The sign was
Your brother will tell on you.
A stone of Sijjeel, the petrified clay, (3)
Stones like rain.

Rain for the waste lands,
Rain for the waste heads,
Rain of stones.

O, sparrows,
O, hands that have not yet grown feathers,
So they can fly,
Until when do you want to hasten your last run?

One night I saw him.
Mothers were bringing their children to him,
To kiss them, one by one.
I said to him, Sir,
Are you not marking on every child?
His martyrdom medal?
But he continued kissing them and crying.
Their fingers held his face
Like birds' wings.
One of his companions touched my shoulder, whispering,
Brother,

Have you counted how many medals they tattooed on his cheeks?
As much as those he will live,
As much as those he will die,
Until they have a homeland of their own,
Where they can have graves, and homes.

Oh, the Time of prophecies!
I have vowed my blood to a sky winged by sparrows;
I spend my lifetime singing for them,
Saying, they will grow up one day,
Certainly, they will grow up one day,
Carrying in their beaks love and pollen,
Making their nests a homeland,
Not emigrating except to it,
Not propagating except on it.
Was I mistaken, my homeland?
The cub becomes a wolf.
The asps become serpents.
But the suckling sparrows remain sparrows, my homeland.
Yet, what shall kill me,
Is that they no longer carry pollen,
But they carry blood in their beaks.
Blood turned into pollen,
And stones became
Ornaments, in the palms of the damsels.
O, Time of sins,
O, Time of sins.

A stone of Sijjeel,
A stone in the face of this generation;
Then, a stone on the enemy.

The game started,
You were looking, my homeland, smiling,
For your children in every quarter,
When they began, carrying the stones.

Did it occur to you, my homeland?
        That this Time of pestilence,
        That this Time which eats prophets,
        Is desperately looking for good news,
        That voice shall come to it from God,
Girded with stones?

The Times of liars are over now.
The time of calamity is over.
And over is the time of connivers, who
When you look into their eyes,
Their eyes are busy with the nails,
Or mumble something with the retainers…
        O deceivers of your conscience,
                The children hands are Ababeel birds. (4)
                Their stones are fire Sijjeel.
But you left their beaks alone fighting the elephant.

While Abu-Righāl (5)
Was leading Abraha people,
To their homes,
Like sparrows out of their nests
Children were snatched out of theirs,
With the stones, in their hands.
In the eyes of every mother was a cry,
        That could make the stone cry.

The tribal winds did not storm.
The island sands are still asleep on their hillocks.
        Healthy sleep!
What can Ababeel birds alone do now?
        When their stones are different from those stones?
        And the tribal Time is different from that Time?

Who has seen Abraha?
Who can tell him now, before he dies?
That Abu-Righāl

Has now found a road to the House of God,
 Beginning from Beirut!

Our villages are extinguished,
The water-springs in all our villages are postponed,
Except the wells of anger,
Except these black spots, in Arab lands.
 They are all ablaze.
On them, and to them, every door is locked!

Hurl, hurl,
You, children's hands.
Hurl, you children.
The history of the land of prophets
Has found protection, in your fingers.

Hurl, hurl,
You, children's hands.

A stone of Sijjeel
A stone, on the face of this generation.
Then, a stone on the enemy.
O, my country,
Everyone is looking for a camel in the waste
But the House,
Has the children to protect.

(***Al-Rai daily, Amman, Jordan, 8-12-1989***)

Notes:

1. Year of the Elephant: Traditionally, the year 570 CE, when Prophet Mohammad was born. In that year Abraha, the Christian governor of Ethiopia built a church in Sanaa, the capital of Yemen, and tried to encourage the Arabs to make a pilgrimage that church, and to discourage the Arabs from making a pilgrimage to Makkah, and the house of God there. But one of the Arabs refuse, Abraha led a great army to attack the Arabs holy place, using the elephants in his campaign. But the campaign failed, yet the year went down in history as the year of the elephant.
2. Karbala': The holy city of the Shī ‘ite in Iraq.
3. Sijjeel: The petrified clay stones sent by God on the army of Abraha, which stopped him from attacking the house of God in Makkah.
4. Ababeel: The birds sent by God to drop the Sijjeel rocks on Abraha and his army, as we read in the chapter of 'The Elephant' in the holy Qur'ān.
5. Abu-Righāl: An Arab tribesman who led Abraha to the House of God in Makkah, as he intended to destroy it. Abu-Righal fell dead just before he reached is intended House, thus becoming the first traitor in ancient Arabia, and the Arabs stone his grave traditionally.

Nocturnal Prayer

Iraq, because you are
The initiator, the inventive, and creative;
Because the tears of God
Fall with the blood
Shed from your bursting wound;
Because you are the endower;
Because you are protective;
Because the pulses of your valiant heart
Knocking at Heavens' ascents,
To open the gate of light,
For you I write,
Until in these lines God will shine,
Then all the sheets will be removed, O, Iraq!

(*Salāman ya Miyāh al-Arḋ* Baghdad, 1986, (*Greetings, Waters of the Earth*)

Over-Proud Homeland

Between the warmth of unity with death,
And the shivering fingertips,
Between your voice and tempest
There is a flashing shot;
        If I dodge it,
        If I open a pass for it
        In my blood,
All my time will then engage
And I stand upright
And upright stand my Times!
Homeland, alone in what love you endow,
        Up to martyrdom,
        To death or birth
        Does this bleeding moment lead?

Frightened is my language,
You said, 'your trigger is your heart,
Place your finger on it,
Then shoot, my heart will shoot with you'.
        And upright I stand,
        And upright stand my Times,
You said, 'the one who offers love may offer death.
In the stormy rupture moment,
Martyrdom is the whole quest,
When the moment is ripe'.
O, over-proud homeland, over-proud homeland!
I have adored you a path to love,
A path to the Lord,

A path to the language of the heart,
In the revealing moment.
But you have not given me
A moment in my life,
When you were not present
Between myself and my self.
Have you seen a torture like this?
You said, 'unity with poetry is a voice,
With God is death,
With love is loss,
And you are past childhood.'
Then you formed my language the way you liked.
Then I reached manhood,
And achieved my middle age,
But I still have
The taste of beaks on my lips,
The sparrows' flutter in my lungs,
I began lisping in middle age,
And uttering like prophets in childhood,
Forcing myself to be the sacrifice and the sword,
At the same moment.
Have you seen torture like this?
Every path your lovers follow
Is purgatory, at the start?
And purgatory at the end.
And we come to you
Our souls on our hands,
Begging…
Have you…
Have you seen torture like this?
Between two obscure seas we were vowed.
Our beginning: a wave we cannot grasp,
Our end: a wave we cannot grasp,
The entire catastrophe is the life-straits which lie between.
Was it mandatory?
For waters to meet, across our tragedy?
Leafy shades of sadness,

What miracle can allow the heart?
To ooze out into a spring,
To convey the course of its birth
To the mouth of its destiny
While pulsing with love,
With all the arteries, bleeding.
          Frightened is my language,
                    I know I have stolen a moment of fear
                    For which I have to dearly account
Where can I have it concealed?
          I have written a statement of fear
For which I have to painfully account
How can I absolve it?
This is a time when every moment
Bares its chest,
For a bullet to go through.
Who could help a soul to defend itself?

(*Salāman*, p.23)

Colocynth Time

For you alone I can lessen my soul,
For you alone I bow my head,
For your glory alone;
Drunk, I raise my cup,
Brimful with my blood.
Here is my pen,
To exhaustion overburdened with you,
Stamped with your name,
Till lifted are these sheets.
O, you resident between my eyelids,
O, sovereignty!
You are the eternally living;
In your name we begin,
And your name is the last we utter,
As we lie dying.

In the name of Iraq,
        I smash the seals on my bloody voice.
I have what weighs me down,
        Even the unseen I have named,
                But what I have cannot be named.
Angry, are you?
                Of what is my anger?
Or afraid?
        What could I fear?
                I have approached grief at every bank
                And quaffed death till it ran dry.
Hurt?

By all the Arabs.
But I shall continue sowing all my questions, as mirrors,
So, you can see your faces, you captives,
Hoping the foreheads perspire in shame,
So, the sins may be washed off.
My people are victims,
My children's children are victims,
And all who give birth to the end of time,
Are victims too;
Yet, I threaten their killers
That my people are listening,
Then flow the flood of death.
I turned around,
To see my people listening and laughing!
O, sadness,
Chivalry prevents to turn around,
At the moment of death.
But it is a sorrow we cannot resist.
We have never charged anybody with a favor,
Or held answerable, for the burden of dignity.
I swear, if either of my hands were caught up
By my dress, while death is rife,
I would cut it and say to my other hand:
Now you are alone, facing death.
Oh, bitter Time
Oh, colocynth bitter Time.
We have borne you till the ascent of patience
Turned slippery.
Every dawn we open our eyes
To see all your rivers different,
Every river comforting its course all day long;
But with the nightfall,
You hear the creeping of water-steps,
Moving far.
O, Time of thieves,
Time of dubious faces,
And quicksilver eyes, that cannot settle.

The land of educators became the land of usurers,
And people
Drink from a destroyed cistern;
Eat from poisonous trees.
Voices intermingle, so you could not tell
The voice of the oppressor
From that of the oppressed.

Suspicion in the fingers.
Suspicion in the lips.
Suspicion in the eyes.
And those besieged by the dagger looks,
Gleaming from the side of a mouth, smiling,
Know
That they were tied by their arteries,
They were besieged by blood,
Deceived that it was their own,
That they were to their mortal points tied.

Whither can the land-lily depart to,
Carried in Palestine soil
On board ships?
All foreign countries are gloomy
When you enter them, as a refugee.
What will you be my homeland?
A poster in a shop-window?
A chat in coffee-shops?
A show room
Where passers-by step in for a minute,
Perhaps to avoid the rain?
Do you carry yourself, my homeland?
Whenever the Earth shrinks,
To look for a refuge?
Who, in refuge, can collect a homeland?
My country…
How can I carry your winter-sun, Baghdad?
To the refuge lands?

The palm-tree pollen has a childhood season,
        Where shall I start it?
You who are carrying your bags' dust,
        Have you carried a homeland in them?
All stations are sorrow, where handkerchiefs wave,
And trains whistle in departing.

My homeland…
        O, non-departing joy,
        O, non- departing pain;
        You may break the rib,
But your love stops it from tearing my lungs.
That is why I die for you.

O, you who are carrying your guns on board ships,
        The entire oceans yield
        To a passing shadow of a Palestine rivulet,
        Full of orange perfume,
        And an olive-branch, echoing singing sparrows.
Do people kill their homelands?

Who can prosecute the stabbed?
Whose blood has overflowed and prevailed?
Who can blame the one who turns around,
At the moment of earthquake,
To see himself alone in the darkness of death,
With no help,
And tell him not to insist,
When you, alone, to face the impossible,
As killer…or killed?
Alone you bear the brunt of your steadfastness,
So, every horror should rise after you.
The boats know that colocynth is their cargo
        That a corner for crime was prepared by our folks,
        That all daggers were sharpened,
And the hands that waved for the boats
        May not wave again.

As if I discern Tal-al- Zaʿtar crying, (1)
Descry Ṣabra sheering off all her braids and cry
I hear the wind hissing:
O, children of Palestine,
Your uncles' knives are approaching,
Stretch out your necks silently,
The uncles' hearts are tender,
        If any of you cries,
        They weep…

Plague on you,
You, eaters of your mothers' breasts
You, buriers of your daughters alive,
Because they do not offer their breasts to the alien,
A thousand generations later
Bones will be dug out of their graves,
Dead bodies will be asked,
A thousand generations hence,
The future comers would be questioned,
Even the grave-stones,
Then, even the vicious laughter will be asked
Which is its mouth?
        The children will pay for your crimes.
The children will pay for your crimes.

***(Salāman,* p.33)**

Notes

1. Tal-al- Za‘tar, Ṣabra, Shateela: Lebanese Maronite, Syrian army, Zionist forces…Massacres against Palestinian refugee camps in Lebanon, in 1976, 1982.

O, Colocynth Rage

Iraqi troops were ordered to stop their advance on the Golan Heights, 1973

Now, lift up your faces
Let every eye
Measure the distance
Between it and the roaring iron;
        Between it and the clotted blood
                On the armored vehicles,
                        And on the troop-carriers' hoods.
Let every eye measure the distance
        Between it and manliness!
O, you who are closing your doors, over your fear,
        Open them.
O, you who are closing your doors over your grief,
        Open them.
Every drop of light that touches this iron, anointed with blood,
                Then touches you,
                Will open up a vein in your bodies,
                Tearing its covering flesh,
                Asking:
                Why did they return?
Every drop of light that touches this blood
                Clotted on the armored vehicles,
                Then falls in your homes,
        Will burst out now into a banner,
        Which, whenever the wind blows,

Will spray blood on your faces,
Shouting:
Why did they return?
It is the rage, coming now like bitter colocynth,
Bearing death medals,
Bearing its insistence in the grating armored carriers on the land,
Bearing its insistence in the wounds of the cannons,
Lifting their necks,
In glory,
In rejection of your grief.
Open up your doors for the gust of heroism and bitter colocynth rage.
It is the honour, wearing its blood,
Crowned by death,
Whose cannons' necks are forcefully bent away from their fields?
Forcefully, the earth clings to the tracks,
Roaring, with anger, and kicking them.
Forcefully, the roads now bear the weight of this iron,
And the weight of rejecting those great wounds,
For fear they become mere medals.
No pretension!
But it is the banner, fixed at the top of triumph
Pulled out of its roots,
And thrown at the feet of the aggressors,
For defeat to step on, gloating.
No pretension!
But it is the Arabian honour, resounding across the island,
From the depth of Asia,
From the depth of Africa
In the throats of these cannons,
Muted by the silencing order.
All cannons are about to turn on themselves,
And shoot their volleys!
No pretension!

Helpless is the wound,
Oozing, with bitter colocynth rage.
So, open up all your doors.
It is the truthful promise
Coming now from the fire field,
Bearing its glories to the almost shivering streets,
Bearing its glories to where there is no hope
For the blood, or death, to be asked.
Who dares ask blood and death?!
Here it is
The big question bouncing before your eyeballs,
Peeping from the cannons' nozzles,
From the armored vehicles' hoods,
From the tracks chewing the earth in a threat,
From the gazes of wounded lions,
The glorious lions provoked, upon the iron.

O, children hands, fluttering in the nights,
O, their war-songs,
O, the cheers of our women,
O, faces with tears and love joy, flowing on them,
As they were running barefooted in the nights,
At the march of their troops,
Pouring into the streets, towards death.
O, people's joy,
O, people's rage,
O, its love,
Rise up in awe,
All roads
Are in awe, for the weight above them,
In awe, for feeling
That this bitter colocynth blood
Should one day return.
That this bitter colocynth blood
Must one day return.

[***Complete Works, I, Baghdad, 1991, p.519-524***]

His Very Last Words: O, Iraq

For fear your stabbed heart may suffer my pain,
I shall now fold my pages over my wound.
In you I spread all my life, as a banner;
Now grant me a hand to fold my banner.
How often I have dreamt to die in you, carried
By a welter of light and darkness.
My folks, friends, poems, scattered
On the funeral, voices without words,
Except Iraq, calling me, and here I am
Waking from my dream, at the remotest spot of land,
To see people, not my folks, or my language,
And see the soul blunted and incised.
I die in you, though my lung is severed,
You, who blame me about the Iraqis, do not blame!

*****

Of Love

You Cannot Restore What Was

Two eyes closing, chasing out all dreams;
A passion, diminished, then disappears like dreams,
As a pulsing heart that slept.
Do not search in his eyes for what you will not find.
He does not want you to see a wretch in his face,
Whose dreams are but clay?

Do not weary your eyelids, as despair has covered his eyelids.
He cannot see, though your eyes are in his!
You cannot restore the faith that was
In love, in conscience.
You cannot restore what was.

Your eyes overflow with feverish-gleam,
It is your so-called love.
Lately it settled in his side, like a poisoned knife.
Today you came back, to ask his eyes of what was gone.
Was it but love that died?
O, the failing conscience!
You will not raise but despair into that man.
You cannot restore what was. 1952

(***Complete Works, Baghdad, 1991, p. 312***)

The Taste of Beaks

You taught me
        That some lips have a stigma
                Like those of the roses,
When kissed, they fructify,
        And in the maid, flourish every promise.
You taught me that some lips have a world
        Different from ours;
And a language, other than these languages.
        I swear I have experienced girls,
But I have not found lips
        That can summaries all lexicons,
                Between inhalation and exhalation
Without uttering even a single letter!

O, your lips,
        O, fragrance-wave,
O, your tongue,
        The sparrows' throbbing,
                The taste of beaks.
I used to watch their nestlings,
        Seeking protection.
And their beaks are in my mouth!
Picking the bread,
        But picking me too.
I follow their beak,
        Its desire,
                And startling,
O, childhood times!

Your tongue does what the beaks do,
What sparrows' hearts do?
My heart throbs.

O lips that kiss me and captivate,
Smile for me and captivate
And whisper to me a language I cannot see,
Yet, I do not understand anything else.
I yield to you all that is left to me, after sixty years
Of suffering and love.

(***Poems on Love and Death, Baghdad, 1993, p. 119***)

Elongations

Your face will redden more when I believe it.
Your eyes do not lie.
        So how can I deceive a cloud about its water?
                When it rains?
How can I avoid two curves?
        The color of my blood,
When they meet
        The heart throbs between them,
                Trying to find a spot for its arteries!
Your face will redden more.
        You know that I believe its redness,
        And believe more,
                When I see the seagull's neck dropping to the left
And loosen its treasures on the shoulder!

I watch your dozing eyes behind the glass,
        And the daze of the lips
                For excessive piety,
                        Or excessive excitement!

I remain following…
All worlds extend,
        Distances, time,
                The multifarious neck
                        And your lucid limbs,
Where the waters trickle to the heart domain
        Which I leave

As wings sprayed by water
Flickering
And the soul flickers.

Oh, God…
Who can guide me to your impossible way?

(***Poems on Love and Death, Baghdad, 1993, p.116***)

A Reading into Sea-Waves

When I glance at your eyes,
I learn that skies chose a face,
For planting their stars!
I learn that seas have no limits to their depth.
Perhaps the shores of all oceans,
Were an eyelid and mascara jar!
O, you, glittering in the eye and the sea
In the dress, the eye, the sea!
Are the skies related to these eyes?
Who reflects the color in whom?
Neither the sailing ships,
Nor the aeroplanes,
Nor my heartbeat
Knew their way,
And the distances are blue,
Your eyes, the sea,
Your dress, the sea,
The clouds, the sea,
O, God!

(120 Love Poems, Damascus, 2007, p. 17)

Aquamarine Seas

When aquamarine sea laughs
        All seagulls
                In flocks fly
                        Radiantly.

The Galaxy throbs
        The water throbs
                The heart thr…
How did you encircle the aquamarine sea with mascara?

A night forest
        With two aquamarine starts in the middle.
Who would believe?
        That two springs
                No lifetime has seen their equal in greenery
        Are glittering in the midst of night?
And me,
Stunned, contemplating,
        Listening to the flutter of fleeing seagulls,
Then rise all red roses in your cheeks.
        O, bashfulness that intoxicates the soul!
                How can you join?
                        The stars throbbing,
                                The clouds glitter,
                                        And vine tears,
In two eyes, like the flux of aquamarine?

(120 Love Poems, Damascus, 2007p. 20)

Something I Have Not Lost

I still remain, so do not think
That of other than you I do not sing;
For despite my misery,
I still remain, like my friends,
For the land,
For simple people,
For the entire world… singing.

Do not lament what has died of me;
Nothing died except some assumption
That I dreamt of a baby girl,
Playing in a peaceful house.
If I have lost you,
The entire life is my folks and home;
My fellows' children are my own,
I shall love them as I love
My dreams of our brilliant baby,
My love of your innocent look.
I should remain in my night,
And for the image of our baby, sing.
If I am quiet, do not think
That I am finished,
Because I drudge, so shall not sing. 1957

(***Complete Works 1, Baghdad, 1991, p.147-8***)

Birds' Wings

When I kissed your eyes
I roused the sparrow-flock from sleep,
The chirps devoured my face,
The beaks tickles were on my lips,
And the taste of beaks
My blood became wine.
As I was like a child
And the world painted on your lips
A breast- nipple
I realized the way to my weaning was long
And I went too far…
Who said that love could be satisfied?
When I opened my eyes
I saw the sparrow-flock drowsing
A vein on the supple neck was pulsing
O, birds' wings do not shiver,
My heart is a vow to your sleep
I kissed it,
Then I dozed.
The morn was watching me.

(Complete Works I, Baghdad, 1991, p. 496-7)

Daily Burning

As if you were illusion- haunted,
As if you did not paint your eyes in his
As if,
No use, and we apologies a thousand times
Then we resume to dally.
          And we are ruptured every time
And because your love was nothing but assumptions
We said it may,
          And it may not.
We said,
          Like the others,
She will pass
          To be remembered, as a face of others' faces.
Two days, two weeks,
          Sorry.
We have become…
As if you inspired an illusion,
As if you did not tattoo your lips on his,
As if you're waiting, and the way so long,
Was nothing but waiting.
Watching the way so long,
Was nothing but invention?
You dressed in what he liked,
          Because he had liked it;
You showed him your nails' paint,
The one he liked.
Like a cold white kitten, you used to rub
Your face on his button - loosened chest,

Shivering,
And humming,
Then you left.
The road never was,
Nor your steps on the road,
Nor your little smile,
Nor the innocent sigh,
But an assumption,
Mere assumption.

(Complete Works, Baghdad, 1991, p.545-7)

Signature

When you enter my tent,
The sand turns grassy.
Fresh leaves grow among the wood crevices.
The words rush up to you,
    They scatter themselves into letters,
    And race up to you to read.
When you enter my tent,
What comes over it?!

(Complete Works I, Baghdad, 1991, p. 549)

A Third Signature

The waves broke up all the ribs of the ship;
The sea dallied with Sindbad;
But when it lit up a harbor for him,
        The sea lost its shore.
You…
        O, harbor that escaped when it beckoned me for a
        second,
Wait!
O, seas of eyes,
        Wait for us,
        As we are departing, tomorrow.

(Complete Works, I, 1991, p. 552)

The Gold Chain

The gold chain,
Fumbles with the crystal fingers,
The crystal fingers' worry fumbles with it.
It rises to the lips,
It settles in the spots of flame,
They let it off.
          The gold chain drops down,
It creeps into the turns of light.
The eyes meet,
They smile,
          The eyes drop down,
The look breaks
          The feelings expecting assumptions meet.
The entire unknown gathers
          On the chain of gold.

(Complete works I, 1991, p. 553-4)

An Invitation to Everything

A passage, among the fires of your eyes,
Beckons me.
The shores are shunned when the water burns.
All oceans I shed for that call which beckons,
From between your eyes.
Would the impossible islands open up their harbor?
A mast glittering on the waves,
As the water splits away from it,
Will come to you naked,
Till you discern among its saps,
The reverberating breath, naked,
So the water is embarrassed by its nakedness.
O, passage, bounding among fires,
Would be impossible islands open up their harbor?
It is a sign to defy.

(Complete Works, I, 1991, p. 555-6)

End

Like a brilliant star falling,
Like a tearful eye,
Between its lashes, a drop fell.
How can you look for a star in the fog?
How can you look for tear in the sand?
How…?

(Qaṣā'id fi-lḥub wa-l-Mowt)
Poems on Love and Death (Baghdad, 1993, p. 5)

The Sin

Who of us, now, is the other's destiny?
Your eyes, both, are dripping,
And the candle, settled in its cup,
Also drips.
But,
I am the melted one, arrogant in his silence.
Who of us, now, is the other's destiny?
--I never dreamt that you…
--What?
--… Think of me!
How can I make her see that, now, there is wine
In her cup?
And that I am infatuated with her, thus?
A child!
I contemplate her like a god contemplates his sin.
How can I make her see that, now, she is
Too young for my courting?
That, now, she is
Too old for my courting?

(Complete Works, I, Baghdad, 1991, p.540-1)

Regret

Thanks to the chance,
Long remained the trick with us,
Regrettably!
Like a porcelain statue falling,
Turning into fragments in a moment,
Like mirrors cracking,
Showing an image that wounds the eyes,
It cracked.
The dream for which we lived two years,
Cracked.
Long remained the trick with us,
Regrettably!

(***Poems on Love and Death, Baghdad, 1993, p.7-8***)

Dew

Everything she has is dewy,
When I touched her,
Leaves grew in my hand!
    Her voice… Her two eyes,
    Her neck… Her two lips,
All the water the sky hid for tomorrow,
A cloud,
By a cloud,
Between her sides flourished,
If she laughed,
    Or walked,
        She rained!
How dewy!

(Poems on Love and Death, Baghdad, 1993, P.15)

Luxury

Laden with clouds,
Laden with rain,
As if the starry rays,
Over her two eyes passed!

As if the ocean pearls,
As if the oysters all,
Brought her their luminous shells,
To choose from this a smile,
From this a tearful look!

O, her hair… Oh gold,
O, her mouth… Oh, flame,
O, branch,
          Delicious fruit,
Water and fire!

If a breeze approached towards her,
O, God…her dress!

If she but moves two steps,
Her foot prints would shout:
Why?
          Where?
She keeps moving among the roses,
All day long.
A void remains,
Waiting remains,

For her return
Laden with clouds,
Laden with rain.

(Poems on Love and Death, Baghdad, 1993, p.213)

Fire Lancets

You are killing me now,
        These fingers… Their tips,
                Are fire brooks, behind her, racing.
All my arteries explode,
I feel my skin cracking,
A fire cloud spreading in my ears,
                        And my eyes.
They invaded every duct,
        Burning my nerves, one by one.
You are killing me now…
                Do you…
Do you feel my soul's response?
        With all its pain?
Does this palm of yours hear the pores crying?
        Under its fingers?
Profession?
        Or feeling?
The entire world turns with me,
And I feel nothing but these lancets,
        Going deep,
                Deep,
                        To the last blood spring in my veins,

Numbing my skull,
I wholly plead with them,
While they slaughter me
If they could penetrate my body
To open among the wounds
An exit to my soul suffering…

(*Poems on Love and Death, Baghdad, 1993, p. 47-9*)

*****

Of Other Concerns

*****

Sources of Light

O, clouds,
Thicken as much as you want over the humans;
And when you squeeze the rain,
Over the houses roofs,
Remember that light does not die,
And that all stars
Grew up in you;
And that the moon
Opened in your heart a stream of kindness
To send warmth to the tired. 1952

(Complete Works, I, Baghdad, 1991, p.224)

A Drop of Sorrow

A home for the fears of this world is my heart.
Who knows your frontiers, O, fear sparrow?
O, fear kingdom,
Home for pain,
        And my love carries me.
I depart from you,
And depart in you.
What cross extending to the ends of earth is my departure!
O, my heart,
O, bird exhausted by hovering,
But is still pulling his crushed wings in all parts of the world.
O, treasure of fear,
O, drop of sorrow,
        Throbbing on the world Cross,
O, my heart!

(Complete Works, Baghdad, 1991, p. 339)

Do Not Knock on the Door

Do not knock on the door, you know they have departed,
Take the keys and open, man!
I know you will go to check on their windows
As you used to do, and follow where they entered.
You watch the food; did they sleep without eating?
You turn off the lights, you wish they have once done!
You have a thousand prayers that they should have forgotten
So your eyes could be graced with them before sleep.
Do not knock on the door, as when you did,
They used not to come down, and you lost your temper.
They would giggle, you could be cruel and curse them.
But secretly, you were alight with love and pleasure.
Yet when they opened the door, and you met them,
Your tears would flow from excess of love.
Do not knock on the door, you have been doing so for two days,
But, oh, you of thick grey hair, they did not come down!
You will see the dumb rooms with turned off flights,
And their belongings were carelessly thrown about.
Their shirts, books on the shelf, tapes
He beds, where they left them, and did not care.
These were very dear to them, as their eyesight.
But now they are covered with lines of ants.
You will find toys, of which they argued with you

To keep for themselves. Now they left them and departed.
Take them, why do you kiss them, then, and cry?
Those kisses are the dearest they desired.
O, tears of the eye… Who, among you, this evening
Will share with me, as the moon of sorrow is full?
Here, my wide and spacious house looks at me,
But every door in it has a hasty lock.
As if a voice is calling me, and I hear it,
O, guardian of the house, the occupants will not arrive.

(***Poems on Love and Death, Baghdad, 1993, p. 165***)

Beginning of Sorrow

Everything is foggy:
My laughs are foggy,
My tears are foggy,
All our days
Are sunk in fog.
Is it because the tops are remote,
        I cannot see,
                Or because,
My eyes fell into the sand?

(120 Love Poems, Damascus, 2007, 67)

Insomnia After Sixty

When will the dawn break?
There, you are leaving your bed,
For the third time,
You turn on the lights in your living room,
You read for an hour
And return to your bedroom.
You know that sleep will not close your eyelids,
As long as her image is between them.
You fool yourself,
If you apply your head to the pillow
It is four o'clock,
The distance between you and the dawn,
Is far still.
Two hours of tense worry lie
Between your bed and the study,
And, between your bed, and the tired clock.
The clock hands drag themselves
As if mountains were on their back.
So, when shall the dawn break?
O, God!
You are past sixty years,
And you still cannot sleep for pain.

(120 Love poems, Damascus, 2007, p. 145)

The Everlasting Drowsiness

O, hope of my suffering heart,
O, world of my aspiration,
In my loneliness and alienation,
O, my solace
When ailment presses on my breath,
And consumes my withering youth,
Distract me, all around me darkened,
And drowsy are my eyes.
Distract me, I have despaired of the world,
And I have no hope of return.
O, dearest of hopes,
Would I drown in your looks?
Before I am gone!
A premonition of departure is what obsesses me,
So could I but see you once before,
I am for over gone!
Who would plead with you, for me?
If now my suffering could not plead?
Who would plead, if all around me?
Went away,
Neither brothers, nor even friends! 1949

(Complete Works, I, Baghdad, 1991, p. 300-1)

The War
[Selections]

Yellow defiles your hands,
        Your eyes are full of blood,
Flare up, destruction, that you are,
        Yet nothingness is what you are.
Explode in fire flames, and brands,
        And top with clouds of smoke,
And thunder: no era has gone,
        And no new one has shone.

*****

Death, O war, not a field you left,
        But where the farmer left the plough;
By fire fields were tilled, and there
        Victims' heads like seeds were sown.

*****

Ferocious despots' heresy,
        For dollars barter human blood,
Korean mission you fulfilled,
        But what, except your shame, you gained?

*****

Don't quench the fire, till rage calms down,
        Or into caves the chests would turn,

Then raise a bust in every cave,
        For peace, and what a morbid peace!
That lofty monument, with flame,
        Is liberty statue, or free men's jail? 1950

(Complete Works, I, Baghdad, 1991, p. 109)

The Lethal Bows

Standing among the orbits,
Like a spent meteor.
Every star has its spear,
And it has its wound,
Before it is gone.
Alone, the silent, constant, unmoved,
In the midst of the nebula,
Standing,
And the orbits have their bows inflamed,
Meeting,
And panting,
At his birthplace.
He chooses,
Then he raises a bow as wide as the sky,
He centers himself,
The entire earth becomes a string.
The bow bends till the ends touch.
Then he shoots in the outer space.

Thus he used to play with the star,
Shooting it through his lethal bows;
A complete round,
Then he pulls it, a tremendous fire,
Disappearing under his feet,
And he is like a spent meteor
Silent,
Constant,
Unmoved,

In the midst of the entire nebula.

Frightened am I of my language,
Whenever I stir it,
Its dormant histories it awakes,
Its metaphors,
And cloudy similes.

(Poems on Love and Death, Baghdad, 1993, p.55-8)

Stupor

Baghdad quietly burned.
As if eyes could not see
Except smoke, and ashes.

Smoke.
Two months we used to get up,
Every dawn, hearing the fire siren,
But we see no fire gleam.
And like sparrows, on brands with no fire,
Our little children flutter.
Then they sink into the depth.

Silence,
No sound,
No breath,
No cat mewing,
No glance, no whisper, and no arm
Extending
To welcome
Or to bid farewell.

Smoke.
All faces, all betray disgrace.
Tiny hedgehogs,
Creeping in the ways,
Burning without light
Without a thing disturbed
Except the smoke and ashes.

Loss.
A sea of stupor.
And all of Baghdad is dying,
But not frightened are all
These which creep along the ways,
Like human beings, shape and form. 1953

(Complete Works I, Baghdad, 1991, p.171-3)

Apology

When I complain to you,
I complain to the man in you.
You have never ever been an arid land,
And you are not to blame,
We have not sown,
We have not irrigated,
But we complain of hunger,
And curse the sterility in you,
How much aversion and ingratitude
You suffered from your children!
My good homeland,
O, wreckage…1955

(Complete Works, I, Baghdad, 1991, p.180)

A New Year Wish

She asks me to make a wish:
        What would I want?
If I were to be born anew:
Young lady,
        Every single day
I am born anew
I die and you
And after every death
I dread my other birth
I wish if…
        But I am born despite fear
So the big game would reach the end.
Young lady,
Between my daily birth and death,
I wish for once
I could be born like all people,
Once born child;
        Another time,
Die as a child,
Not understanding this big game.

(Complete Works, I, Baghdad, 1991, p. 538-9)

Neglect

A queen once
Put a nightingale in a cage.

He spent the day singing,
He spent the night singing,
And the cage
Was leafing around him.
It became a thicket,
It became a forest of entangled trees;
        And he continued singing.
In the morning
The Queen found him at the bottom of the cage,
Dead.
In his beak, there was chip of wood.

(Poems on Love and Death, Baghdad, 1993, p. 41-2)

The Last Visitor

Without appointment,
Without disturbing my children,
Knock at the door,
I will be in my study, most of the time,
Sit down for a while, like any visitor,
        I shall not ask,
                Neither what,
                        Nor wherefrom.
When you find my eyes full of tears,
Take the book from my hand,
Put it back, please, quietly,
        On the shelf where it was.
And when we leave
        Do not wake up anybody in the house,
As it is the most catastrophic sight
Which the eyes can see
Is the faces of my children when they know…

[Won the 1984 Stroika prize]
(Poems on Love and Death, Baghdad, 1993, p. 51-3)

Worry Late at Night

Afraid, are you, when you think of death?
Or tired?
Your only care, morn and eve, has become
To return to the blood- pressure meter,
Worrying, watching its ticks,
While it is counting the beats of your heart…
You know you have loaded your heart
More than it can take,
Then you are counting
And questioning.
Tired you are my friend.
You should have watched your heart
Thirty years ago.
Can this directed instrument
Do anything now,
But frighten you?
Fifty years,
And your heart is massacred by its pulse.
You did not place a watch of your calm
Or your madness
One day on its throbbing.
And now you are watching its beats.
It is the rhythm of all the years
Which you ignored,
Now it is coming off beat,
Because you spent your life playing
On your heart cords,
Not thinking once of their corrosion.

Frightened are you?
Or tired?
Your heart is still beating, my friend.
Let it, at least
Decide how to end its off beats.

(Poems on Love and Death, Baghdad, 1993, p. 59-62)

Civilisation

You all may summarize the world,
You may land on Mars.
But whatever you do,
You can never make
A drop of light in a warm dawn
Weaken, and grow old…
Explore however you will
Pull the future string till both ends meet,
You will find in Sumeria
The first wheel in history,
Running behind its prophecy
The last wheel in history.

(Poems on Love and Death, Baghdad, 1993, p. 66-7)

Writing on Water

How beautiful it is to write poetry!
We follow the soul waves,
The words' sails,
We run with the watercourse,
And cross to the other bank.
We laugh, cry, love, and bare ourselves.
The noblest in us bares itself:
The soul
The wounded child
Inside us bares itself,
Splashes in the water.
On the surface he writes names,
Effaces names,
For fun, and memory
For fun,
And memory.
For memory!
What illusions!
Three days later
All our stories become memories.
How painful it is to write poetry.

(Poems on Love and Death, Baghdad, 1993, p.203-5)

*****

Visionary Poems

*****

Whence Comes Your Calm at this Hour

Voice:
Because I scattered my body,
Among the people;
Because I bore their suffering;
Because I used my own name,
Voice:
Because the distance, between the bullet
And the heart, is short;
Because the one who blocks the road,
Between the killed and his killer,
Is the witness and the killed?
I became the impossible witness of my Time.

Voice:
Cursed is he who holds up
The trunk of the killed for his killer.
Cursed is he who cheats a person,
Away from his eyes,
Or his hands.
Cursed is he who trusts a wolf in pastures.
O, generation of vipers,
For two thousand years,
I have been looking for my head,
Among shoulders and heads.

How many bodies like mine are searching?
A little girl:
Johanna, take a lip from me. (1)
A little boy:
Johanna, take an eye from me.
A voice:
Johanna… Guide my shoulders to my head.
How many bodies like mine are searching?
How many bodies like mine are searching?
Dedicated to sorrows, am I, tonight.
Dedicated to open my doors to the exile birds,
To offer my eyelashes to a drowsiness,
Whose end I do not know,
Gloomy is my soul.
Gloomy are all my wounds.
Gloomy even the earth that wraps me, tonight.
Ah, for the moments which precede your great waking!
Consecrated tonight am I, to the greater worry.
Consecrated tonight, to be alone with death.
And death tonight will be alone with me.
I, the severed- footed, trying my balance point
Tonight, alone.

Full of silence, and full of the unknown.
And full of all non-possible things tonight.

And you thought you knew.
You saw people dying, so you know.
What do you know of a language?
Not spoken except by your death tonight?
If you could but stand, you leprous footed,
At that moment,
Without swaying or falling on your face!
Who knows?
They will say out of fear,

They say of despair.
You know you are dedicated, and you accepted,
And people say, and say…

If you could run to death, to shorten the way,
To shorten the betrayal!

Consecrated am I tonight to sorrows.
Consecrated am I to be slaughtered tonight.
I am searching for the direction-point of my death.
It is a pity to be killed between doubt and belief.

You were told: turn your looks towards the west horizon,
And look for a star.
If the soothsayer's prophecy proves right,
It will tonight appear on the west horizon,
At midnight, look,
If the star leans to a corner on the horizon,
And settles, shivering,
And if the sky turns yellow, and you could see
A sky of sulphur,
Closed like metal,
Where sleeping breaths exhale like white smoke,
And when on everything prevails a drowsiness like death,
And no moan is heard
Except the pulsing of the frightened star on the horizon,
Except the fall of your legs, in fragments on the ground…
Turn your face towards the west horizon.
The soothsayers have made a true prophecy.
A black stone will emerge
Swimming in a somber glow,
If it shoots its gaze into your eyes,
Then limit the size of future death,
And ascertain the direction-point of your slaughter,
Do not miss it.

And make sure to be the master of your death,
So it does not beat you, and you will be killed, vanquished.
But if it passes by without turning around,
You would implore for another lifetime, to meet it.
And you will not be allowed that.
You implore to be killed,
But you will not be killed;
To live,
You will not live.
Woe on you!
And wail and woe on you
If you wink,
If you are distorted by fear,
If defeated, challenge with despair.
Small is the size of death, which will play its game
With you, then.

Perhaps if you see it, you will find a harbor,
For your faith.
Perhaps you will not despair,
Or find solace.
Perhaps. Perhaps. Perhaps.
I am numbed,
And was distanced from my worry…
When the night reaches its middle…

Between me and you, midnight,
There is a distance, where I die a thousand deaths,
And live.
Between me and you, midnight,
There is a wake, if it calls on me
Who would guarantee that my hand
Will not shiver with the cup,
Making me doubt that I will drink it!
Horror, of which our old women whisper,
Or make hints, when asked,

Implore God help, and turn down the looks.
Our damsels laughed at you,
And I saw scourges in your eyes,
And saw the smiles escaping sideways,
Turning into blushing, bashful quivers,
And you recited a prayer,
Then asked for forgiveness for us, the naive,
Us, who did not see the bloody star, and do not know
The meaning of a bloody star,
Rising, on the western horizon.

Whence comes your calm at this hour?
Had you stretched out with what remained of your lifetime?
You would have turned flabby, with wider cells,
So you would not feel what goes through
your flesh,
You refused to cut through your lifetime, except in depth.
Let it be!
Contemplate how your knife chops up all your arteries,
While delving deep to the last moments of your
lifetime.

Whence comes your calm at this hour?
You who are lurking for your death,
Or for a cause, to make your death riper in your eyes.
-- Oh, you afflicted man,
Other people consecrated a star,
But you were consecrated to a star,
And there is but one night between you, as
you know…
-- I know…
--They tied the string sevenfold; you
When they take off their hands
The six knots will untie themselves
You know.
-- I know.
-- Look, there is but one night between you,

Which is all the space;
And between us is a knot,
Which is all the distance.
With my teeth, I tried it.
The lifetime worry I gathered in my nails…
-- We know.
-- With my silence, I resisted.
-- We know, but it is one night.
Ah… Who can haunt patience, with a protruding knot?
Round its tonsils?
Ah, who can haunt silence, slaughtered between two stars?
Each promises him death?
Every day
I imagine myself dead one way,
Then I refuse it.

Should I carry my grave,
And tour with it,
Asking people
Who can tailor a death for me?

O, Lord- like body,
This is a hand denied by all prophecies,
Imploring you to receive it.

I feel for the sides of all nails in your live body,
So grant my hand the courage to touch the same spots,
In my body.
I know that nails in my body will rust.
I know that I will flutter again then calm down.
No flesh remains,
No sign remains,
And here you have been for two millennia, my Lord,
Every night the flesh covers you,
But with the break of morn, you are naked.
For two millennia, my Lord, you are eaten, and silent.
Is it not time now to be angry?

To cry, now?
For all these deeds that handed you over,
To silence, to…
-- Oh, you, swaying in the sphere of death,
Are you alone?
--Who is asking?
If you have a witness with you, now,
Let him vouch for you.
-- I have no one but myself.
-- Step aside then.
Let him advance who came with his witness.
-- Oh, voice
O, language which turned my hair grey.
O, call of the paths which led me astray.
O, language which killed me,
Be you my witness.

You refuse, I know,
But I did not expect my neck to bend like this.
I came carrying my skin.
Death has tattooed even its nails- roots.
Does its statement satisfy?

I came carrying my eyes,
You know they have turned white,
For the long gazing of death into me,
And me, into it.
Does their presence satisfy?

I have a pouch,
Since my mother told me that nails
Bear witness on doomsday,
I gathered them one by one.
Can their statement satisfy?
O, voice. Oh, you…
Thus?
I do not even have the right to claim my death?

I had as many witnesses as my pulse- beats,
But they could not prove I was alive.

Who would now lend a witness, to one looking for his death?

O, Yahya,
You have witnesses as many as the hairs on your head,
So leave your head and do not look for it.
If it returns to your shoulders,
Deny it then.
Ask to have it severed.
Asked to bring a death witness.
Yahya, leave your head
O, Yahya, leave your head,
O, Yahya leave…

Here is my cup flowing,
And I am still at the beginning of the night.
Which roads did you take that did not allow?
Your death the chance to choose, Sir?
You filled up your cup,
Yet not a single drop spilled over,
But I,
With half a cup, overflowing early at night…
The difference, Sir, is so great
It is my support
It is midnight.

And the bloody star which,
And which perhaps…

And the premonitions, Master,
Each one is an age,
Each premonition equals an age of death.
Which roads did you take?
So the language of death curtailed its details in you?

O, cup,
 You are damned to be drunk to the full,
 So do not shiver.

O, eye, do not blink.

We push fear away by death,
 Or push death away by fear,
 That is our problem.
All prophecies fail to name a dead without a witness.
 So I am postponed,
 Postponed to live,
 Postponed to die,
 Postponed, postponed, postponed.

O, you dead without a witness,
Your death is rejected now.
So pick up the rest of your shrouds,
And follow me to this midnight,
Then die as witness on each other.

O, you dead without a witness,
Follow me to this midnight,
Follow me to this midnight.

Notes: **Yohanna: John the Baptist, his name in Arabic is Yaḥya, a name which has its roots in Ḥayāt: Life.**

The Voice
I-Prophecy and Travel

Reciters closed their throats,
The ancient scrolls were folded,
This is an age which has no ears,
Whoever rains, let him rain petrified clay,
          Now the earth does not imbibe water,
Severed were the necks of early vows,
          One dodged the sword of age,
It is the voice.
          This is a sign I know,
                    The thunder hangs down,
                              And the earth imbibes it.
Black sun rises,
No water remains in its course but for one day,
          Then it changes course.
Children are born without names,
          Then the voice arrives.

It is the call,
Whoever is touched by revelation?
Let him not reproach or escape it.
          For this is an age where even the devil
Proves his prophecy right.

A neck dodges,
Silence, the Sultan perched in the world's bell
          Is swaying at this moment,
          As the neck has picked up the bell rope,

And wrapped its tonsils.

Death trees,
Grow ear-leaves,
And hearken.

This is my first acquaintance with doomsday,
I open my eye,
It shoots like lightning.
The world skin enters into the flesh,
Things become transparent.

The horizon folds its wings,
Then opens its bow.
The voice will come
From the bottom of an eye, across the open bow.
The voice arrives,
So, trees, grow leaves.
At this hour a Lord rises,
Leaving a stoned age,
Extending to a stone-thrower age.
Ears open before it
And tongues are tied.
He brings letters for which eyes turn white,
And stick to the forehead,
Flow as a spring,
Or flourish as firebrands.
They obliterate names, and dig other names
Into faces.
Who can hear this voice?
Has found himself a name to carry, at the Flood.
But who is not reached by the voice,
Or he is reached by the voice, but cannot hear,
Or stuffs his ears by his fingers and cannot hear,
Woe on him.
Those ramble about the land with no names.
They knock on doors which do not open.

Those who wonder about the fires with their faces,
Begging for a blaze,
They dangle into the waves with extended necks,
Imploring to drown,
But the water withdraws.
They stretch down,
But the water withdraws.
Those remain a denied call,
They have no name to be called by on doomsday,
To be happy or doomed.
Their stickler would say:
We have not heard a voice.
The liar would say,
The voice did come,
But I did not imagine I was the one meant;
It did not tarry so I would ask something.
Their hypocrite said,
The voice did come,
Knocked on my door,
And called me.
Woe on me!
My feet did not help me to follow the one who answered.
Say everyone is approached from far.
People would die and come back;
Die and come back.
But you
Are not among the living, or the dead.
Blessed be the alienated,
Blessed be the exiled,
Blessed be the trunks planted in the land of death.
My voice shall reach them.
Now I am opening the book of Revelation,
I am extended along a white space,
On a white sheet.
Let all world languages drown,
These are waves where no words can sail.

But the dream- vision
Glides on them, a sail full of the voice
It is the revelation.
Can the ears of those stretched on the beach hear?
I am reaching Saba'
Bringing you some news.

Whoever believes?
Let him pull out his shoulders from the beach sand,
And follow me,
Or escape his shoulders,
And follow me.
If you disbelieve,
Then wait for the overwhelming sand- flow.
Here I am on my other bank,
Overlooking across the stream,
To tell you what I find...
Alone
Mirrors of silence spill over
Glitter...
Exhaust the soul
Nothing can wound it.
My step fell
And silence broke under it
I did not move the other foot

I halted...
Distances stretched before me,
Smooth and glossy.
What a walk if the steps would now take off their feet!

My alienation flourished,
Distances pillage my eyes,
Pillage my arteries
I stretch out, almost dismembered,
Pulled by the foot- root settled in its flesh.

O, eternal purgatory
To you I carried my flame,
I, the Mandaeanized comer, (1)
The herald, the diviner…
A sheet of silence crashed,
It wounded me…
I said nothing,
I did not let any feeling move.
My wounds were bleeding
With clatter oozing out.
I was rising slowly,
Then I found myself afloat
Flimsy…
Like a line of light
Moving away.
My remains were gazing at me.

Oh, stream, glittering between the eyes and their lashes.
Heavens are smashing their gates' seals,
Galaxies move aside,
A meteor rises from among them,
It glides down.
The bow opens out.

Here I am, full of your waves,
O, stream, trickling between the eyes and the lashes;
Coming,
My throat is full of the voice.
O, trees, where death has clustered
Its black branches,
Flourish,
As the banks of sin raise the ears,
It is the voice coming…

Note: (1) Mandaean, the Sabaean religion of a minority in the south of Iraq.

II- Iram Before the Flood

O, ears across doomsday beach,
I see a land,
Every vision above it has its scepter broken
Who has permitted now these pillars to rise?
Who called Iram (1)
To be planted facing my eyes?

The vision lies, as it did not leave its place?
Or is the wave that sailed with me restored me?

O, meteor that all galaxies avoided its way,
Wait!
Were it a scroll you learned, do not read.
I have vowed a white trip no eye has sailed.
If you, meteor, have hung it
Across the universe orbit,
You were not mistaken.
I have entered a virgin Iram,
None, but this firstborn nebula,
Has alighted on its soil.

From my footmarks, bows rise up,
And tour the universe,
To meet, at the point where I stood.
Every moment is the entire time.
Every step is the scope,
And it is nothing…
Here every comer loses his features.

He is seen as a child,
Then, as an old man.
Forefathers and children differ
In his face, in a moment.
Then they all disappear.
He reaches me,
I see him without face,
A sign is planted in his hand.
I see him going away with it,
And doomsday din is between my eyes and voice.

O, ears, be in the windward of the voice.
I see what no eye has ever seen.
I remembered myself as a child…
But at the moment of remembering
I saw me
Passing before my eyes a seven-year-old boy,
My dress itself,
My favorite recited poem.
I read it,
Then I disappeared.
I was not a phantom,
My footsteps are still there.
The voice I heard
I recognize.
I shall not disbelieve the vision,
Though Noah's folk did.
O, thirst of rivers and banks,
I lay my neck on a sword blade,
To catch the swordsman's look,
During the slaughter.
I take a handful of this land soil,
And the fires neigh out of my palms…
A sign I know.

Iram,
Come to me, you of revered fires,

My twin of burning branches;
A sadness I recognise.

O, ears,
The curse stripped off its skin,
Iram
Is smashing the seals of its gates,
Coming out to me, naked.

Some folks came running without feet,
They saw me…
          They turned off…
I turned them over,
I cannot see if they have faces,
          But I see
                    Spots of eyes, noses, mouths,
On the soil.

I asked them,
They did not speak.
But I heard a thunder from their heads,
Rising in my hands,
Imploring me not to touch its fear.
It said,
          We left trees with branches escaping their trunks.
It said we left every mother bird eating her nestling.
We left the wind…

O, ears,
I see a land opening up its mouths
          Drinking thunder
Its belly was torn
I see seven spikes (2) rising up now,
Beckoning to the seven cows, (3)
Ate them,
          And the dugs vanished…

Around me were folks busy
With a slaughtered she- camel. (4)
Their palms raising her trunk to her legs,
          Whenever it gets there,
                    The trunk tilts again.
Woe! It is Thamood, (5)
Thrilled by this she- camel until the last day.

Thamood, Oh, Thamood,
I bear, for you, the everlasting curse.
If you believe that Ṣāliḥ (6)
Is not himself the she-camel;
And that he will return,
Will return, Thamood,
          From his long journey,
With one she- camel followed by another.
I give my head as a price,
          If you did not try,
                    Once more, to slaughter that she- camel.

Into the silence hall enter some people,
Carrying their graves.
It was shouted at them:
Stop.
They turned looking at each other's face,
And they set down the graves,
          Then they buried themselves.

It was shouted at them again,
They stood up,
Carried their graves, and left.
It was shouted at them…

O, worlds with severed tongues and hands,
You have eyes for fear,
You have legs for fear,
So run, do not ask me where to.

O, destiny that I am,
O, destiny, its companion is the first to betray it.
In this land which eats its prophets,
Eats its saints,
In your name, in this hell, I begin doomsday.

O, ears,
Towards me their graves-bearers approached.
Their eyes had severed eyelids.
Their lungs were hanging on their chests.
        They dropped their eyes on me, silently.
        They passed me by without turning…

I spread my call behind them,
I saw my voice hanging out of my mouth,
        And falling within two steps.

O, you grave- bearers…

They vanished.

        The voice kept its place, within two steps…

Curse on your ears,
Curse on your steps,
I came closer to my voice,
I placed my head near it,
And found me of usurped power.

I close my eyes,
        A huge eagle, like a cloudy dream, appeared to me.
        It hovered over the world, wounded,
                Crossing the horizons,
                Gushing in blood.
                        Roaring thunder,
        Then falling, as a bloody tent.
I felt it breathing its last, among my ribs…

I see a land playing indecent,
I see youngsters courting her,
She dances among them,
She strips naked,
They fall on her nakedness… She laughs.
The kick her nakedness… She laughs.
They blindfolded her,
She danced though blind.
She turned among them, stretched out her hands,
They spit in her hands,
She halted, cried, and wiped her palm
On her nakedness.

They turned around her, laughing.
They spit in her other hand,
She folded her hand
Her tears flowed, and carried them off.
The bow spread open to its ends;
Saba' stretched out her hands…

O, ears,
    A finger sets between my eyes, I cannot see,
I am being pillaged.
-- O, You, crossing death river,
This is a soil no eyes ever touched before you,
So, spread out your eyes.
-- Oh, herald of Saba',
    I am disobeyed.
        Is my voice my voice?
            It is suspicion, is my eye my eye?

The finger made two turns
I saw its shadow across the orbits
    Then down it fell
        And settled between my eyes.
I open my eye,
    It sprang a lightning behind the bow.

O, city gravestone,
O, ‘Ād, (7)
O, Thamood,
I have found a passage.

Skins penetrated their flesh.

Oh, city corpses,
I have found a passage,
So, follow me.

Woe on you,
Their skins harden.
Their skins grow inwards.
The flesh was forming,
The bones were forming,
The soul became a skin.

Woe,
They died into their base…
O, my folks, take off your skins.
Perhaps I can see the shiver of life.
O, my folks, open the flesh when fresh,
Insert your fear roots,
Your love roots,
Worry roots, hissing under the bones.
O, my folks, grant me your truth…
Do not inherit the tears, but be a witness, you ear.
That the Lord has wept,
My eyes bleed is blunted, the vision is blurred.
Who can warn this Lord that an awful dam
Called Ma'rib (8)
Is collapsing before his eyes, drowning his vision,
So he would see nothing.

I am at the frontiers of Saba'. (9)
O, ears, the lightning is broken,

The night is beastly black like stilt,
Every comet I set apart gouges out its eyes,
And plunges into a well.
A bloody roar is creeping from every corner of the earth,
        And it swallows the voice.
I, the suffocated by my tears,
By the blood thickening in my throat,
Call you to pick up that wild voice.
        It is a vision forming into a living body.

Let your trees flourish into ears,
Branch out into arms,

With every arm, opening its palm into an eye.

        The flood has come to you,
        The flood has come,
        The flood came…

Notes:

1. Iram: an extinct city, traditionally built by Shaddād ibn Áad, between Ḥadramout and Ṣan‹a in ancient Yemen. It is mentioned in the 'Chapter of the Dawn' in the Holy Qur'ān, as 'Iram of the Pillars'.
2. Seven green spikes, eaten by seven dry ones: dream of the King which needed interpretation, as related in the 'Chapter of Joseph' in the holy Qur'ān.
3. Seven fat cows eaten by lean ones: in the same dream of the King as related above.
4. The she-camel: belonged to Ṣāliḥ, the Prophet sent by God to the people of Thamood, which they slaughtered, and were punished as a result.
5. Thamood, an extinct nation in ancient Arabia.
6. Ṣāliḥ: the prophet sent by God to the evil nation of Thamood.
7. Áad, another extinct nation in ancient Arabia, mentioned Thamood in the Holy Qur'ān.
8. Ma'rib: probably the most ancient water dam mentioned in history, in ancient Yemen of the first millennium.
9. Saba': an ancient kingdom in Yemen, 1200 BC-275 CE.

III- The Flood

A grain of sand is pushed by a drop of water,
A molar tooth with a drop of blood
Springing from its hole,
A larger grain of sand
          Is pushed by a larger drop of water.
The pulled molar tooth grows,
Its hole grows,
Its blood grows,
Ma'rib is collapsing,
          It is creeping.
                    The Flood came…
Sand in the eyelashes,
Sand in the soul,
          And sand in the clothes,
Sand in the doors,
And whistling…

Meteors collapsing,
And locust of fire,
With millions of fangs,
Falling and flying,
The desert spreads out,
          And runs, fleeing.
Every tiny grain of sand grows into a skull,
Rolling,
          Followed by the fangs.
The grate clatter of sand confounds the ears.
The Flood came.

The Flood came.
Came the Flood…

A lump of flesh, mixing hands, feet, and intestines,
Mouths gaping, with gushing blood and sucked milk,
The colour of tar.
The flesh lump creeps,
Chewing the earth surface,
The earth intestines,
And the earth graves,
So you hear the crying of the dead all night.
When the sun shines, both eater and eaten hide,
So you cannot hear the sound.
Two arms as wide as the universe spread out,
The tide rises,
Two legs appear
With nails and rods,
A head dangles,
Crying, proceeding,
Followed by a thousand crosses.

Out of the midst of the waves necks come out,
They stretch out,
They flutter with their heads above the lump,
With gaping mouths,
With gaping eyeballs,
They look deep into the universe,
They shriek deep into the universe,
Then they return to the lump with bent necks.

The eye- shells float,
Cry,
Then they vanish into the bottom.
I feel, by my hand, for a path in the creeping bloody body.

A hand, the size of an egg,
Severed from its wrist,

Holding a breast,
And the breast oozes milk on the bloodied fingers.
I stumble,
My lips stuck to a slice of flesh,
I lift it,
A spark of lightning shone in my hands.
The slice became two, joining near the mouth.
The larger one was mixed with plaits,
The smaller was a hair- lock.
A cowry pierced its head,
Hanging over the forehead.

Countless, like sands, float eyes
Crying,
Then they vanish into the depth.
The waves rise and tumble down,
Naked bodies run,
Overwhelmed by waves,
Covering the feet,
Covering the legs,
Covering the necks,
They prevail…
The bow opens,
Saba' beckons, across the open bow
Woe on me!
If I had my legs with me,
If my flesh and bones!

The lump rises as volcanic foam
An aperture opens,
A reed forest rises bearing a white body, with gorged eyes.
A cigar dangling from his lips, touched the chin.
The waves sank.
The borne body bent to the bottom.

Ma'rib is creeping from every corner of the earth…

The flood was pierced.
A black lump of flesh peeped, crying.
The waves mixed, and I could not recognise of the crier's face
Except two torn eyes, dripping in blood.
I saw black hands, pierced into the black neck,
Until it turns blue and the blood bursts
From the two corners of the mouth…
The black hands dragging it to the depth,
To be covered by the lump.

O, ears,
I am still wading in the Flood,
Picking up flags of Saba'.

I see willows talking,
And old palm-trees weeping,
And sparrows…
The earth is full of sparrows,
Worms coming out of them,
Eyes and beaks…

I see severed breasts,
Oozing in milk… over deserted cradles…
Wailing;
Palm tree- trunks,
Each holding its severed bit,
And the pollen was flowing.
They are overrun by the waves,
So the palm- tree tops float,
And float the birds,
And float the breasts,
And all vanish,
Nothing is left but bare trunks,
And empty cradles rocking above the water…
O, eyes that cannot see,
Ears that cannot hear,
Who can tell you, now,

That the mirrors of the entire world,
Show nothing but a bleeding wound
Or a tearful eye…

I am lost in the lump,
Not knowing where.
Extinguished is my soul,
Extinguished are my eyes.
Suddenly devil heads,
On rafts of clay,
Cut through the lump towards me.
They reach me.
These faces I know.

The waves rose, and encircled the palm trees,
Until all the clusters spat blood…
I almost yelled,
When a pile of flesh covered my face,
And a crying of a woman,
Holding the head of a suckling baby,
Looking at me, moving its jaws.
I wiped the lump off my face,
And looked at it,
To find bleeding flesh,
And suckling fingers shivering,
Looking for something to hold.
So I fell to the depths…

How much time
Has passed on my death,
Until it could restore me to my voice?
Who, I do not know who.

When I awoke,
I was in a clay raft
Around me were humans like devils heads
I lifted my head

They dropped their eyes on me,
Full of light.
Woe…
They are the grave- carriers.

They smiled when they saw me
Running with them
Carried by my grave…
I knew it…
From the touch of the clay.
Its formation was like my own,
My smell… My memory… Even my arteries
I felt them carrying blood,
Between my body and its clay,
I shouted…
The voice echoed in the passes of the space,
The entire world grew ears.

I turned my eye,
Symbols and names,
Were slowly rising on the water surface,
And, at the range of vision,
The Flood was ebbing.

It is me, who, in his hand, carries a sign,

IV- Iram After the Flood

Who is, now coming out of dooms day.
Searching for Saba',
Even death I asked about your path,
But it hid itself away.

Was Time Frightened?
By my shape?
          Of the Cave dynasty am I,
                    Or of the flood?

Then,
          I am in a Time which is not mine,
In a Place, which is not my place…
                    Or is the flood
Another plot
For a newer sleep,
Where blood and fire took the place of ice?

Iram…O, you greatest earthquake in history,
Most horrendous cave in the world,
If this vision were to be true…!
The last breaths of the flood
Would eject what they have swallowed now.

Woe…
Silence at eyeshot range
Destruction at eye-shot range.

Silence,
And destruction…
Human corpses…
Cat corpses…
Dog corpses,
Corpses everywhere,
Perforated by worms,
Gnawed by rats.

And stones…
At eye-shot range, stones.
Here are human remains.
Here a house remains…
Petty creatures,
Killing each other…
Eating each other,
Jarring among the rocks.

I approached them…
They blocked the way,
And stopped…
Their eyes are lightning…
Their doubts are lightning…
Their skins are needles.
I called them…
They rolled over,
Each resorting to a stone.

I retreated, vanquished…
They came out of their holes.
They looked right.
They looked left.
And, ran away.

Oh, remains of Iram.
I came carrying my voice,
Between my death and my death,

Looking for Saba'…
But you blocked my way.
An enemy am I,
Or a friend?

All eyes are fear…
All are accusation.
There is no breath…
And no speech.
I saw your eyes orbiting in the sockets,
Your fear slaughtering you, and not leaving.

I saw your blood flowing…
Your homes collapsing.
I turned my arteries into rivers,
And came to you, sailing on my grave.

They came out of their holes…
And looked in my direction.
They looked at each other, silently,
Then they returned behind the hillocks.

Oh, remains of Iram,
Perhaps I cannot see what you can,
But I know that eyes
Do not deceive the looker,
And now I see the entire catastrophe.

I see the frightful looks,
Secretly leaving their lashes,
To look for a reason for desertion.

I see God weeping,
And chivalry weeping,
And see all your necks being twisted,
Between fear and doubt.

O, my son… Oh, my daughter… Oh my home!
O, remains of Iram,
Do not eat your brother's children.
Do not slaughter a children's father,
Like his children do.

Let none of you see a man dying
To try his dagger on him,
Even if he saw his killer stabbed,
O, people of Iram.
Let him not be cruel,
And slaughter his own witness.

As if I see rivers of tears…
Trunks with dislocated ribs;
And see ships with bloody sails,
And see people thirsty,
See them hungry.
I see every tree trunk a cross,
Every person a Jesus,
And see all my folks departing.

O, remains of Iram!
As if I see all that is in my blood
Propagating of my blood…
Bloody stumbles my voice,
Among these headstones.
Everything is dark.
I stumble among sins…
Among victims:
The captors before the captives,
The weaned before the weaning.

Then I glance at the bow opened,
In its depth, a herald of Saba':
O, traverser of death-river,
Do you have the same voice,

Or the news was barred from you?

All existence moved away,
Now I am alone,
To make a decision alone.

Who would believe my passion?
Would believe that I crossed the orbit,
And saw what was before me,
And saw what was after me?!
O, victims of Iram,

When you wake up a witness for you,
Once more,
Gouge out his eyes,
Fetter his hands,
And stuff into his ears,
Your voice alone,
With no competitor…

O, victims of Iram:
Every voice has a sign,
And has a domain,
In which he centres,
Beware against saying to a voice
Though weak:
Stay in this orbit.
It will exaggerate in refusal,
Or exaggerate in yielding.

A Dramatic Poem

Al-Ḥorr Al-Riyāḥi

الحرّ الرِّياحي

Dramatis Personae

Al-Ḥorr Ibn Yazeed Al-Riyāḥi	An Umayyad general
Abu-Ḥafṣ, Ámre, Ziyād	Captains in his army
Ḥārith	His son
Yoḥanna,	John the Baptist
The guide	Yoḥanna's guide
Shimr Ibn Dhil-Jawshan	Al-Ḥusain killer
Suhail, Mālik	His men
Al-Ḥorr's Obsession	
Al-Shimr's Obsession	
Ámmār, Ḥārith, Yasir	Followers of Al-Ḥusain
Áisha	Yasir's wife
Sulaim	Their son
Rasheed	Police Commander
of Abdullah ibn Ziād	
Chorus of Children	
Chorus of Men	
Soldiers and others	

ACT I

Place: Al-Ḥorr's camp near Koofa. (1)
Time: Dawn of Al-Ṭaff Battle. (2)
N.B. The voice of the obsession is heard by Al-Ḥorr only.
Al-Ḥorr, alone in his tent

*****

Obsession: It is the moment of silence,
So, let your words curtail themselves,
Shall you retreat, or kill now?
Which of your two ways is clearer?
A scorpion is slashing the night among your ribs,
Its back is corroded, if it spreads out
Your horses will now miss even their hoofs.
The swords do not philosophise their actions,
In the tumult of death. [Neighing]
Al-Ḥorr: Here is the sun rising, the people rising,
The few words rising.
Their letters rising like giants, blinded, mad,
Fumbling, inside you. Which of the two ways is clearer?
Obsession: Your sword had an opinion, which is the edge,
An edge, which is the opinion.
Your opinion and the sword have become two edges,
The humidity of the closer one is touching your head now, O, Ḥorr.

Al-Ḥorr: [To himself] Woe! If your obsession were heard now!

[Enter Vanguard] What is your news?

Vanguard: Good news

Al-Ḥorr: [Joyfully surprised] Did they escape?

Vanguard: God forbid! Is their escape good news I bring to you?

Obsession: The only good news!

How can the chaser see God's cries between the eyes of the chased?

Al-Ḥorr: Then briefly.

Vanguard: I saw their hearths…

Al-Ḥorr: Dying out?

Vanguard: The ashes are still warm there.

Al-Ḥorr: and you followed them?

Vanguard: I did.

Al-Ḥorr: Describe them to me.

Vanguard: Few hoof prints, few footprints,

Mostly of children. I thought they distorted their way.

Al-Ḥorr: Have they done so?

Vanguard: No, but I was misled by their children's footprints,

And by their excessive branching.

Al-Ḥorr: Hmm…m.

Vanguard: [Laughing] They felt themselves out of death reach, and went playing.

Al-Ḥorr: [Angrily] Were you brief?

Vanguard: Your pardon, my Prince.

Al-Ḥorr: Enough! Did you catch up with them?

Vanguard: Yes.

Al-Ḥorr: Where are they now?

Vanguard: At two leagues on the way to Koofa.

Al-Ḥorr: Tell the men to saddle their horses.

Vanguard: At your orders, my Prince. [Exits, to leave Al-Ḥorr alone]

Al-Ḥorr: [To himself] they felt themselves out of death reach,

And they went playing. You felt safe,

They were mostly children.

The smallest wound is older than them.

You felt safe… They were few,

The right among them shouts but once, then it falls on its face.

Obsession: Woe! Ḥorr, you order to saddle horses!

Did you make peace with yourself?

Here you are, with no saddle on your horse except obsessions.

No arrowhead in your sheath, except obsessions.

Al-Ḥorr: I know that my sword has an answer when asked now,

I know that my horse knows all its duty.

And I…

Obsession: you fool yourself, O Ḥorr. You have the sword,

But its grip is in hand not yours!

Here are the reins of a thousand horses held now by your hand.

You control all their wind wards,

But your horse's reins are not among them.

[A beam of sunlight falls on Al-Ḥorr's hand as he was blowing away the sand].

Al-Ḥorr: [to himself] It is the sun.

Her every grain of sand is different from the other.

Has your soul's darkness a star?

Has this mixture a beam that sets it apart?

If the waters could make a promise,

I would have opened a road to this first with my dagger.

[Calling] Mas‘ada!

Vanguard: [Entering] At your service, my Prince.

Al-Ḥorr: Ask Abu-Ḥafṣ, Ámre, and Ziād to come to me.

Vanguard: I'll do now [Exits].

Obsession: Then what? Your army is already on horseback.

Your captains are coming. The night's bleeding

Has, still, not sent a single line of light, into your ribs.

The night's bleeding has still not sent…

The night's bleeding has still not sent. [Enter the captains].

Abu-Ḥafṣ: Good morning, O Ḥorr.

Al-Ḥorr: Good morning to you all. Please sit down.

Ziad: And the men on horseback?

Al-Ḥorr: Never mind… What is between you and Ḥusain

Is no more than what it takes the horses to chew their reins but once?

[As they sit]

Obsession: Here you are running away from yourself.

What use is what you told them about the distance?

Now between them and Al-Ḥusain,

If the distance, between yourself and Al-Ḥusain, you do not know?

Al-Ḥorr: How did you leave the men?

Ziad: Curbing their horses, but you could see neighing in their eyes.

Al-Ḥorr: And you?

Ámre: [Rising, unsheathing his sword] Ask these swords

Who is thirstier to blood, us or their edges?

Obsession: Do you see? If you hold of yourself now

What they hold, would you hesitate in unsheathing your sword?

Al-Ḥorr: [As if addressing someone] If I had a proof…

Obsession: What proof is like a sword cracking in its sheath?

Al-Ḥorr: Then they say: Al-Ḥorr squatted licking the pus of his obsessions.

Abu-Ḥafṣ: Did you… Say anything my Prince?

Al-Ḥorr: [Noticing their presence] I was saying…

Obsession: Say, damn you!

Bring them all down to what you brought yourself down to.

Then look at their swords after that.

Al-Ḥorr: I wanted to…

Obsession: Wanted what? Every word you utter now is a sword,

To feel the soft core in your soul like a woman weeping?
Look at the destiny you make by this fear!
Be their master and speak,
Or their slave and your tyranny slave, and keep silent.
Al-Ḥorr: [Lost with himself] But I say,
Abu-Ḥafṣ: We are listening, Prince.
Al-Ḥorr: [Noticing them once more] Do you know why I called you in now?
Abu-Ḥafṣ: How do we know if it were anything but to start the war?
Obsession: How can anyone else know? How?
[The captains look at each other for a long time]
Abu-Ḥafṣ: O Ḥorr, something has been worrying you since yesterday.
Al-Ḥorr: Yes.
Ziād: Order me to cut the desert neck now,
And it will not bleed for a second.
Al-Ḥorr: Easy… I may need your sword for a severer blow.
Ámre: Are you testing your swords today?
Abu-Ḥafṣ: [Interrupting] Ámre…
Abu-Ḥafṣ: Ámre…Quiet. It seems to me that all the swords of the earth
Fail to cut what worries your Prince.
Ámre: But…
Abu-Ḥafṣ: But what? We have to listen, then to obey.
Al-Ḥorr: Easy Abu-Ḥafṣ. If I were to give an order now
Would you disregard it?
Abu-Ḥafṣ: God forbid!
Al-Ḥorr: I have not asked you in to obey,
But I asked you to view with me.
Ámre: So, let us see what you have, our Prince.
Al-Ḥorr: O, Ámre!
Ámre: At your service!
Al-Ḥorr: If I were to wade with you an army of Demons,
Fighting you, but you see none of them,
Would you wade after me?

Ámre: You know we would.
Al-Ḥorr: I know! [He looks at them for a long time].
Suppose I charge with this my sword,
And this my lance, on boys
Who run before me, then fall down,
So their mothers pick them up, frightened,
Running in every direction, then I said:
Charge on them with me, would you do so?
Ziād: Would you do so, O Ḥorr?
Obsession: You do so, O Ḥorr? You do so?
Al-Ḥorr: Find me an answer to this, your question, Ziad.
It is for this I have called you in now.
Obsession: A lie. You lie. Since yesterday
Your cowardice has been in control.
Since yesterday, you have been fighting yourself.
You did not know a thing about Al-Ḥusain army,
Do you assume sympathy to cover your slaughtered glory,
Now, then drape it over Al-Ḥusain?
He accepts your sword as much as you accept
Your shame now, as you lie, O Ḥorr, you lie.
Ziād: Would my Prince allow me to ask?
Al-Ḥorr: Who? Ziād?
Ziād: Yes.
Al-Ḥorr: Have I put a bar between us before?
Ziād: No, my Prince.
Al-Ḥorr: Why do you ask then?
Obsession: Do you deceive yourself,
Or ask to see how much they doubt themselves?
They beware of you, they beware the hand
Of the frightened man, who is alert.
If they feel it is the hold of one sure of himself,
They would not have asked permission.
You know that the hand of fear is destructive,
Yet you will insist on your fear to increase.
This is only the beginning.
You have come to find a hint in every word they utter,
So you double your gaze into them.

Abu-Ḥafṣ: O, Ḥorr! We used to enter into your soul
By the widely open door, without permission.
Al-Ḥorr: And now?
Abu-Ḥafṣ: Now it seems to me that you're sure hers locks and guards.
Obsession: Valiant. This is a language in control of its truth.
So it settled. Show clarity like this,
And say a word, the sun would hold in a spot you decide,
If you clarify the space, between your heart and lips.
Al-Ḥorr: O Aba-Ḥafṣ!
Abu-Ḥafṣ: Yes, my Lord.
Al-Ḥorr: If your companion's soul should remove its locks now…
Abu-Ḥafṣ: By force?
Al-Ḥorr: But by choice, and willingly.
Abu-Ḥafṣ: People would enter, not fearing it, nor far from it.
Al-Ḥorr: [Turning to Ziād] Then ask.
Ziād: What I want? Or what you want to be asked?
Al-Ḥorr: Rather what you want.
Ziād: Shall I be brief?
Al-Ḥorr: As much as you can.
Ziād: [With some hesitation] O, Ḥorr…
Al-Ḥorr: Speak!
Ziād: Are we with Al-Ḥusain or against him?
Ámre: [Surprised] Ziād!
Al-Ḥorr: Easy Ámre. We have to bear the cautery
When the disease is too grave with us. [To Ziād] O, Ziād!
Ziād: At your service.
Al-Ḥorr: A moment ago you were with the army.
Ziād: Yes.
Al-Ḥorr: You left them with neighing glittering in their eyes.
Ziād: That is right.
Al-Ḥorr: They are groomed for the war then.
[Turning to Ámre] And you, Ámre ibn Ábdillah?

Ámre: at your service, my Lord.

Al-Ḥorr: Do you find yourself more thirsty for blood than your sword?

Ámre: Rather, I am more thirsty than they.

Al-Ḥorr: All preparation for war is in you then.

[Turning to Abi-Ḥafṣ] And you, Aba-Ḥafṣ?

Abu-Ḥafṣ: Obedient, whatever you demand.

Al-Ḥorr: This is an army raining victory.

[He assumes the pose of an orator among them]

We are before an enemy coming to destroy crops and cattle

And take our case out of our hands, claiming it unlawfully.

Ziād: [Interrupting] To destroy crops and cattle?

Ámre: But we did not accuse Al-Ḥusain of what you said.

Al-Ḥorr: [Continues, as if he did not hear their objection]

He charmed people, attracted them around him,
They believed he is the son of the Prophet,
And that on his face there was a message not read,
That he is its reader.
He claims that he came with that message as a saviour.
They believed he was all that.

Abu-Ḥafṣ: [Interrupting] But he is all that, O, Ḥorr.

Al-Ḥorr: Eh?

Abu-Ḥafṣ: He is all that.

Al-Ḥorr: I know.

Abu-Ḥafṣ: You know, and you say all you have said of him?

Al-Ḥorr: Do you want me to lead my men to kill Al-Ḥusain?

I will, but to kill him,
They have to believe that this whose forehead
Is stamped over, the one whom they challenge,
With arrows shot in him, is not Al-Ḥusain,
But a man who claims a falsehood, deceives people,
And who will soon ruin them. I shall make them believe
He is no relation to Mohammad.

Abu-Ḥafṣ: But you know that all you said is untrue.

Al-Ḥorr: After we win the war, nothing but this would be true.

Abu-Ḥafṣ: But it is a lie; a lie that makes the listener perspire for shame.

Al-Ḥorr: Woe on you! A moment ago,
All your claims sounded large.
But here you are, if I were to point to any of your swords,
That it is the one to start, it will shiver in its sheath.
You have not killed Al-Ḥusain yet; but here you are,
Afraid, even to accuse him of anything.
Who, among you, will bear the sin tomorrow?

Ziād: Those who led us to kill him will bear the sin.

Al-Ḥorr: And you?

Ziād: Soldiers obeying the orders of their captains.

Al-Ḥorr: Rather, hunting dogs.

Abu-Ḥafṣ: O, Ḥorr! You are insulting us, unfairly.

Al-Ḥorr: But I am like you, a hunting dog, will pant after the game,
Sticking his fangs in its vital parts,
Then, carries it back to his master, as a hunting dog would do.

[A moment of silence]

Ámre: Can we see the point in your opinion now?

Al-Ḥorr: If I could see it.

Abu-Ḥafṣ: The lightning flashes in the darkening cloud, O, Ḥorr

Al-Ḥorr: Look for it, then. Catch any of its fingers,
And let me see my inner self lightning.
I promise you I shall blind my eyes by the light.
But show it to me first.

Abu-Ḥafṣ: O, Ḥorr! You have held all the fingers of your lightning.

Al-Ḥorr: Have I?

Abu-Ḥafṣ: Yes, you have.

Al-Ḥorr: Then show them to me, Aba-Ḥafṣ.

Abu-Ḥafṣ: Am I safe?

Al-Ḥorr: Eh! Why does the sky not grow a thousand paws,
To stick them all in my eyes!
Ámre: Why, my Prince?
Al-Ḥorr: Grant me, other than doubt, an eye to see you by,
A hand to feel you by.
You sow suspicions in all my skin pores,
Then you fear them.
How can I feel safe in my thirst
While whenever my bucket goes down
To the bottom of your wells, the water escapes?
Abu-Ḥafṣ: Could you inspect your bucket, O Ḥorr?
Al-Ḥorr: [Looking at him for a long while] What did you mean, O Abu-Ḥafṣ?
Abu-Ḥafṣ: What you guarded against.
Al-Ḥorr: Be clear.
Abu-Ḥafṣ: You drop a bucket down to the water
While you know before dropping it that it will return
Without any drop of water, on its sides.
Your bucket has an uprooted bottom, O Ḥorr.
Al-Ḥorr: You are trying to…
Abu-Ḥafṣ: [Interrupting] To say that you know that,
But you intended, then you insult our wells.
Al-Ḥorr: O, day of storms and impossible meteors,
Which of your prophecies can be safely believed now?
Abu-Ḥafṣ: I swear if I turned the entire desert into water,
And the waves would overwhelm you to the ears,
You would close your lips under the waves,
Until you die of thirst.
Al-Ḥorr: Then…
Abu-Ḥafṣ: You would say we shall not fight Al-Ḥusain,
Then you would not add a sword.
Al-Ḥorr: [After keeping silent for a while] And you Ámre, and you Ziād?
Ziād: There is enough in what Abu-Ḥafṣ said, O Prince!
Al-Ḥorr [To himself]: What an adversary I am plagued with today!

All your life you have saddled the entire wind wards.
All their reins crossed under you.
Not a horse stumbled when you were its rider,
And here you are [To Ámre] O Ámre!
Ámre: At your service!
Al-Ḥorr: Tell me truly, Ámre,
If I were not a rival to this man, waiting for me
Now, between his grave and the edge of the sword
I am carrying, then who am I?
And what has brought me to him?
Ámre: When a hawk is released after its prey,
Does he question its owner why it was sent after the prey?
Al-Ḥorr: Then I am like what I said, a hunting dog.
Ámre: Rather…
Al-Ḥorr: [Interrupting] Easy, Ámre,
If I were a hawk, I would insert my beak now
Into my chest, out of anger, or would insert it…
Abu-Ḥafṣ: Where, O Ḥorr?
Al-Ḥorr: Into any rock on which it breaks, Aba-Ḥafṣ
Into any rock on which it breaks.
Abu-Ḥafṣ: You, Ḥorr, possess your sword
Al-Ḥorr: I possess it down to its base,
Where I feel it, bending as a rib over the heart. [He rises]
You filled up my vessel. So return to your soldiers in peace.
Between me and you there is a moment,
To approach the water, or dread it.
Ziād: At your service. [They leave and he stays alone].
Obsession: No way!
You, the stickler, will not drink the water
Which they give you, as a favour.
You are searching for your own water now.
Nothing quenches this thirst except your own water.
Al-Ḥorr: If I could find its source. [His son Ḥarith enters].
Ḥārith: Good morning, father.
Al-Ḥorr: Ḥarith? What brought you here at this hour, son?
Ḥārith: A dream that frightened me, O Prince!

Al-Ḥorr: Welcome, welcome!
Our heroes are frightened by dreams at the dawn of war!
Ḥārith: You know, father, I am not afraid of war
But I can hear and see what is going on around me.
Al-Ḥorr: And what did you see?
Ḥārith: I saw you giving up your eyes to the wind,
Your arms to the wind
You have even locked your arms together
So that one hand would wrench the other,
If you tried to unlock them.
Al-Ḥorr: Hmm…m. And what did you hear?
Ḥārith: I heard what you are hearing from yourself now.
[He kept a moment's silence]. Father, I am worried.
Al-Ḥorr: Woe! You worry about whom?
Ḥārith: About a woman whose phantom visited me yesterday, crying.
Al-Ḥorr: Cried on you?
Ḥārith: Rather on both of us, father.
Al-Ḥorr: She is your mother. Did that phantom tell you anything?
Ḥārith: I was lying awake still,
When I heard something which I thought was the wind.
I listened, but the echo was getting near.
I could miss my own face, but not this voice.
A shiver ran through me when the night receded.
I never saw horror like the one in her face.
[The mother's face appears gradually in the horizon
Of the stage, until it becomes clear].
Mother: O my son! O my son!
I know that I shall not see you after tonight,
I shall not see your father.
I know I shall be the most bereaved,
The most tragically orphaned woman,
The least hopeful, the least visited.
But I came to you to protect me from a horror,
Greater than my impending calamity.

O my son! If all the water is bound to recede,
And all this blood is bound to flow,
Do not, you two, be the sword to beat;
Do not, you two, be the sand to soak.
I heard a voice.
The voice [An awful voice is heard from the depth of the stage, As if coming from nowhere]
Al-Ḥusain will be killed
And this sign will remain
All the swords plunged in his blood,
All the sands soaked in his blood,
Will remain stained to doomsday,
Will remain stained to doomsday
[The voice ends and the mother's face disappears from the stage]
Ḥārith: After that, father, I heard them weeping
Al-Ḥorr: Woe… Who?
Ḥārith: All the poor, father, all the orphans.
The sky was splitting with their wailing,
And weeping was pouring all night, weeping.
Chorus of children: [As a voice behind the stage]
Ḥusain, O Ḥusain
O hand-tied, O free-handed.
After you, candles will be blown out,
Tears will abound
We will all be bared, all hungry.
O Ḥusain! O Ḥusain! O Ḥusain
[Crucified Christ appears on the stage horizon]
Christ's voice:
Because I scattered my body,
Among the people;
Because I bore their suffering;
[Christ disappears. Che Guevara appears, killed, on the horizon of the stage]
Voice:
Because the distance, between the bullet
And the heart is short;

Because the one who blocks the road,
Between the killed and his killer,
Is the witness and the killed?
I became the impossible witness of my Time.
[Che Guevara disappears. The Baptist appears with severed head on the stage]
Yohanna: Cursed is he who holds up
The trunk of the killed, for his killer.
Cursed is he who cheats a person,
Away from his eyes,
Or his hands.
Cursed is he who trusts a wolf in pastures.
O, generation of vipers,
For two thousand years,
I have been looking for my head,
Among shoulders, and heads.
How many bodies like mine are searching?
A child: Yohanna: Take a lip from me.
A little girl: Yohanna an eye from me.
A man with a severed head:
Yohanna… Guide my shoulders to my head.
Yohanna: How many bodies like mine are searching?
How many bodies like mine are searching?
[Chorus from off stage]:
Ḥusain! O Ḥusain!
It is a promise, Ḥusain, to follow you on the day of thirst,
Betwixt and between. Betwixt and between.
Woe to those who are betwixt and between.
Neither against you nor with you.
Voice: O land of thirst,
Where the small trees are resting behind the thirst,
I am no longer a ladder
Besieged by the eyes and their ailments,
And by the wounded Time. (1)
Al-Ḥorr: No, you will not be a ladder, O Ḥorr,
You will not behead the Baptist once more,
And will not crucify Christ. [Calling]

O Mas‘ada [Enter the Vanguard]: At your service.
Al-Ḥorr: lead me to Al-Ḥusain camp. [To Ḥārith]
And you Ḥārith, hurry to Ziād, Abi-Ḥafṣ and Ámre.
Let them follow me. [To himself]
I am no longer a ladder
Besieged by eyes and their ailments,
And by the wounded Time.

And now, Ḥusain,
The apex of this sun
Is closer to my sword than your head.

1. These lines are by the poet Fawzi Kareem.

ACT II

Time: An evening, one month after the killing of Al-Ḥusain.
Place: Al-Shimr bin Dhil-Jawshan house.
Persons: Al-Shimr, Mālik, Suhail, of his men.
Obsession: The inner voice of Al-Shimr.
Voice: Al-Shimr voice in Al-Ṭaff events.
N.B. The stage is two parts:
The present: Al-Shimr and his group.
The past: voice of Al-Shimr, his group, and the events of al-Ṭaff.
**All voices and phantoms are heard and seen by Al-Shimr alone.
**In the Act there are two voices:
Al-Shimr's obsession and his voice.
The two voices are separately called as 'the voice' for Al-Shimr, and
The obsession'.
Obsession: Why? Why? Why? Why?
Voice: A hand-palm, the colour of tar, with a white finger.
Were it my palm it would terrify me.
A child voice: Thirsty!
Voice: This calm serenity,
This look of prophetic eyes… I hate.
Long voice: Aaaaah…
Children voices: Fire, fire, fire.
A woman's voice: O my Ḥusain!
Al-Shimr: [Startled from his daze] Who is wailing?
Mālik: Did… you hear anything?

Suhail: Woe… A whole week and this wind does not calm down.

Al-Shimr: [Turning to him angrily] You are all deaf, then
Send someone to find out.
Mālik: O Shimr! You know that we, since… was killed,
Al-Shimr: [Interrupting violently] Who?
Mālik: [Redressing] Since you returned, a month ago,
And as you ordered, we set spies among all people.
Suhail: We ordered that no bereaved woman
Or any sound of weeping be heard, or…
Al-Shimr: [Interrupting] Enough.
A child's voice: Thirsty… [A child crying].
A child's voice: Thirsty, O Ḥusain! Thirsty, O Ḥusain!
Voice 1: Silence this voice.
Voice 2: I will silence it, hand me that water, Ḥanẓala,
To dip this arrow in it.
A child's voice: Thirsty…
Voice 2: Slow down, this wet arrow
Will fill your abdomen with water.
And now, take and drink. [A child shrieks]
Obsession: Why? Why? Why? Why? Why?
The voice: Imāms… All are imāms.
Tomorrow they will overload the Earth with piety.
Obsession: But they are children. What is their crime?
Voice: What is their crime?
Do you think I am distilling this bitterness,
And squeezing it in their throats for fun?
No, shame on me if I did.
But with the blood of their throats
I shall cloud this whiteness,
And force this suspicious finger
To where the colour of the hand on which it grew.
I'll make it black down to the bone,
Black, down to the bone. Black to the…

Al-Shimr: [The voice diminishes, while on the horizon of the stage a black palm

With a white index finger appears. The index finger points to Al-Shimr. He jumps Out of his place in horror and goes to the palm]

Here you are, white down to the bone,
You go through the door and wall,
You will fill my house, frighten my wake, my sleep.
You will grow between my eyes till doomsday,
White, down to its bone.

Suhail: [About to rise towards him] O Shimr!

Mālik: [Holding Suhail, interrupting] Leave him Suhail until the fit is over!

Al-Shimr: [Gazing into the palm in horror] I startled, all eyes, but I am forced,

If your disappearance were conditioned by blindness
I would stick these nails into my eye sockets,
Until all the white pours into my hands.
But I am forced, forced, and gaze into you,
Forced, and trace your colour,
No… It is him, but even my blood startled,
Yet your colour is still chasing me. [As if he is addressing people he can see]

All your voices, all your sighs, all your eyes
Gather around me, besiege me.
Show me your faces, O eyes I cannot see but their sockets
Should I bear your own sins,
When I do not even know your features?
[He turns in every direction]
Who are you two? Who are you two?
Who are you? You? You? Who?
I killed you all? Or do you want me to render one of you?
Can you do other than gazing in me?
Then burst in anger: I killed him, killed him, killed him.

Mālik: [Rising, and holding him] O Shimr…

Al-Shimr: [Continues] Killed him, killed him

Mālik: [Holding him violently] O Shimr, calm down.
Have you gone mad to chase phantoms?

Al-Shimr: Chasing them? I am simply their prey, Mālik.

Mālik: Rather, you are their creator.
You endow them with a power they do not have.
Here we are around you, but we cannot see or hear anything.
Al-Shimr: Have you ever seen or heard a thing before, Mālik?
If you wanted to hear anything, Mālik,
Then find another Ḥusain, and slaughter him,
Then look at your hands.
Mālik: You, who had the steeds shivering when he shouted at them
Now you rain perspiration of fear?
Al-Shimr: O Mālik, Mālik, Mālik!
You taunt one like me with fear?
Bring death before me as a serpent of thousand heads,
And I'll fight it now;
An army as numerous as pebbles, and I'll break into it.
To fight something you see,
A thing you dare, Mālik, to hit, to frighten…
But, to become, day and night, pillaged,
Spellbound by eyes without sockets,
By voices which yell from within my skull when I close my ears,
And this palm, this white finger, Mālik…
Mālik: Easy, easy. Do not give up to delusion.
You are not too young, Shimr, to sever a head.
Al-Shimr: But, what a head, what a head!
Mālik: Dispel your dread, dispel your dread.
[Pulling him back to where he was sitting]
Come with me; I have something to tell you, [As they sit]
To change what we are in.
Al-Shimr: Do you know what he told me when…
Suhail: [Interrupting] Let alone this remembrance, Shimr,
Push it away from you, for a second, to breathe.
Al-Shimr: But he is here, Suhail;
He is here, while I talk to you about him,
I dispel myself from him by him.

Do you understand this, Suhail? Do you?
To talk about your death until it becomes familiar,
To delude yourself that you are not alone?
You trust your fear with a friend, a neighbour?
A man you know? Do you understand this?
Suhail: I do understand this.
Malik: We are more than one person, you know, Shimr.
So, trust us with it, and be relieved.
Al-Shimr: The darkening cloud shakes off its rain,
But I am like the well.
Volcanoes spit out their insides, then they calm down.
But I am like the well,
The more they well out of it the deeper it becomes.
The more they take out to with more water it flows.
Everything will cool off.
But I have the fire propagating inside me.
I spill it, and it rises. Spill it, and it rises. Spill it…
[A knock on the door]
Suhail: Who is at the door?
A voice from without: An old man asking a favour.
Al-Shimr: Bring him in Suhail. Bring him in Suhail. Quick!
[Suhail rises towards the door to open it]
Al-Shimr: [Continues] A month and no one came near us,
A month and no one knocks on the door but the wind.
[An old man enters, looking exhausted]
Old man: Peace be on you!
All present: And on you too.
Malik: Have a seat [The old man sits] may God greet you!
Old man: And greet the house and its owner.
Al-Shimr: If God listens to this, your prayer.
Old man:[Somewhat surprised] God listens, my son!
Al-Shimr: And responds?
Old man: [With more surprise] If the asking soul is sincere.
Al-Shimr: [To himself, bowing his head]: If the asking soul is sincere.

[Calling]: Wahab, O Wahab!

Wahab : [As he enters] At your service!

Al-Shimr: Bring in the food, and prepare a bed for the old man to rest.

Old man: Can I have a drink of water, may God save you!

I am thirsty… Thirsty.

[The word echoes throughout this stage.

It grows gradually as Wahab exits. Al-Shimr looks amazed]

A child's voice: Thirsty. [A child weeping]

A child's voice: Thirsty, O Ḥusain. Thirsty, O Ḥusain.

A long cry: Aaaaah!

Al-Shimr: [To himself] Which call is hotter and more painful than this call?

Which caller has some of your needs

To calm the soul down?

You writhe like the stung with poison raging within him.

O, what a burn that does not abate,

O, horror that ends then begins,

Ends then begins. Ends…

Suhail: [Interrupting] Fear God, and mind yourself now!

You have a guest, so think of him.

Al-Shimr: I was more in need to fear God about this soul.

At that time, Suhail, I was more in need to fear God then.

But I was obstinate. No, that was not obstinacy.

I remember him whenever I was oozing with fear,

And my fear would slaughter the entire earth.

[He turns to Mālik]

Woe to you, Mālik, when your rival is pushed by fear!

Malik: But you were the stronger.

Al-Shimr: How far! I too was misled by this fancy.

I had thirty thousand behind me.

Do you think I was stronger than the entire army?

Or more courageous than all?

The all recoiled, and he was alone fighting with his breath.

And I advanced. I was there victim.

And the victim of all their baseness.

Now, Mālik, I understand why the scorpion stings itself when besieged.

I was besieged by them. They were all delegating me to kill their fear.

[Wahab enters, carrying a jar of water and a cup.

He pours water for the old man].

Al-Shimr [Continues]

And I bore all their fears.

I was one or the fears of thirty thousand,

With this I killed.

Old man: [Refusing the water, amazed] are you the son of Dhil-Jawshan?

Al-Shimr [Turning to him]: Yes, has my shape frightened your heart?

Old man: No!

Al-Shimr: Then why did you refuse the water?

Old man: Another man was more worthy of it.

Al-Shimr: If the other missed it, do you refuse it?

Old man: I can follow suit.

Al-Shimr [After a short pause]:

If you could do us and yourself a favour and accept this water!

Old man: [Surprised] Do I believe that you insist the give water to the thirsty?

Al-Shimr: Drink to believe.

Old man: What wonder!

Al-Shimr: What can one like me do?

Should I carry the Euphrates on my back,

And tour around calling:

O people, do Al- Shimr a favour,

He has come with the Euphrates on his back?

Old man: Do you exaggerate, or make a joke?

Suhail: Woe!

Al-Shimr: Silence, Suhail!

Old man: [Continues] Suppose you did what you truly said,

Who will come near your water?

It is suspicion in the noble nature of your water, Shimr,

A suspicion which made desolate, even the Euphrates.

Al-Shimr: Have I degraded even the Euphrates nobility?

Old man: You gave the people a chance to curse the water.

Suhail: [Angrily] Woe! To keep silent about you has become a choke.

Al-Shimr: Quiet, Suhail. I want to listen to this old man.

A whole month and my body swells,

A whole month and you dress my wound over its pus.

I want to hear one voice to open this wound,

And come what come may.

Old man: Do not blame your two companions.

They know best what you suffer,

But I… am not useful to you.

Al-Shimr: You make me hear myself.

Old man: Suffice is yourself. [Getting up to move]

Pardon me. Fear God for yourself and myself now.

Al-Shimr: O, You! Spend your night here, and eat or drink nothing if you wish.

Old man: I eat remorse if I spent the night here, O Shimr.

So release me of this favour of yours.

I have never seen the face of the man you killed,

But now I feel I can see it [He steps to the door].

Al-Shimr: And how do you feel towards it, my man?

Old man: [He stops and turns towards them]

I feel I am full of water. I feel I am full of water.

[A gloom reins over everybody. The old man reaches the door then turns]

Old man: Do you know what happened to the Euphrates, you son of Dhil-Jawshan?

Mālik: [Sarcastically] Did it dry out?

Old man: No, but I heard a caller rising from its waters at night.

Al-Shimr: Since when?

Old man: Since Al-Ḥusain was killed. Every night he raises this call.

[The clashing of waves is heard]

Voice: O, you sleepers! It is me, the Euphrates,
The arid waste of thirst.
My sentiments are blood, my foam is blood,
And you are all the water. [Sound of clashing waves].
How small I am before you, Ḥusain!
How thirsty I am for you, Ḥusain!
All my waters do not wet a thirsty lip.
And with the thousands of years with rescue their thirsty.
Assign for my water a portion in your future water.
Assign for my past a portion in your future water.
Perhaps I will recover, O Ḥusain!
Perhaps I will recover, O Ḥusain!

[The voice stops. Old man has disappeared. Only the sound of the
Clashing waves remains, diminishing gradually].

Al-Shimr [Astonished]: Has the old man gone?

Suhail: Yes.

Al-Shimr: As if the night has brought him as a quick warning,
Then it swallowed him.
[He bends his head, and sounds like talking to himself]
His future water will come
To restore health to the Euphrates.

Mālik: You exaggerate even in interpreting nonsense.

Al-Shimr: Nonsense Mālik?

Mālik: Times will show us.

Al-Shimr: more than what they have done?
I have come to beg even the insult,
Even the insult I beg.

Mālik: I do not believe my ears.
Who could dare speak when you were in a bad mood?
You encouraged even wretches like this one to dare you.

Al-Shimr: Do you call this one a wretch, Mālik?

You did not see Al-Ḥorr when he charged alone, to fight us.

[A side scene where the voices of the battle are heard:
Al-Ḥorr, Abu-Ḥafṣ and others]
Abu-Ḥafṣ: Is it not enough that you pulled out, O, Ḥorr?
You did not shed of Al-Ḥusain or his followers any blood,
What do you, then, blame yourself for?
Al-Ḥorr: Are you trying to prove my innocence, Aba-Ḥafṣ?
Who led him to perdition then?
Who insisted to bar him
From returning to Madeena and his folks?
Was it not me?
Who stopped him from meeting the people in Koofa?
Who delivered him to these?
Prove me innocent, Aba-Ḥafṣ, if you could.
Abu-Ḥafṣ: He would have been killed anyway.
Al-Ḥorr: Even if thousand swords were to fight for him?
Abu-Ḥafṣ: What do you mean, O Ḥorr?
Al-Ḥorr: It is too late, Aba-Ḥafṣ; we were to date!
I no longer control these thousand swords
With them I could pull down any cloud I wanted
From its top, and bring down to earth,
By force, and say to it: Rain!
With them I could break the back of the wind,
Or let it blow the way I liked.
But I refrained for two hours!
Do you know how long it is to refrain for two hours?
[He hands his shield to Aba-Ḥafṣ]
Take my shield to you. I do not want it.
Abu-Ḥafṣ: O, Ḥorr!
Al-Ḥorr: [To his people] You are all, innocent of my blood.
[He turns to the others] And you, who…
How shall I describe you?
Any word shall I defile with you now
Will stay defiled, up until doomsday.

May God deny you water to your thirsty!
Why did you pledge allegiance?
Why did you send your envoys to invite him?
Then you made him thirsty?
The new handed him and his children to the arrow-heads?
A voice from Al-Shimr camp: Are you repentant, O Ḥorr?
Another voice: You are the one who gave him up,
And well you have done.
Al-Ḥorr: As for my repentance,
It is because in the morning I was the thirstiest man on earth,
And I saw the water, but did not drink.
And because in the morning I was in control of all your necks,
If I became angry,
But I surrendered to grief, not to anger.
O scorpion issue!
One day the night will clear up
And come the flood
You would be answerable even to your fingertips.
Your last will curse your first.
You will say we were deceived.
You will say we were grieved,
You will say, and you will say.
But you led yourselves until you extinguished
One of God's lights.
Woe on you!
I was an enemy and dared not shed this blood.
Voice from the camp: And now you became a friend? [Laughter]
Another: O people. Al-Ḥorr returned repentant to Al-Ḥusain.
Al-Ḥorr: But it is a debt.
A voice: Hurry up then.
Al-Ḥorr: [Drawing his sword] Here I am.
Here I am, with death before my eyes,
Catching both my feet and hands,

In my neck there is a debt, and what a debt,

Which now I will pay back to Al-Ḥusain! [He tries to leave].

Abu-Ḥafṣ: [Calling] O Ḥorr! Wait a while. You wanted water.

Al-Ḥorr: [Leaving the stage] Far from it.

Al-Ḥusain is water. Al-Ḥusain is water. Al-Ḥusain is the water!

[The scene disappears]

Al-Shimr: I hate him.

Mālik: Why?

Al-Shimr: I saw him torn to pieces, cast on the sand,

He was in the waste of thirst,

As if there were two raising clouds in his eyes.

I hate him. I hate him.

Mālik: [To Suhail] Have you seen his killing, Suhail?

Suhail: I saw all their killing.

Mālik: How did you see them?

Suhail: They were only a few, who managed the death of an entire army.

Mālik: And Al-Ḥusain?

Suhail: [Startled] Mālik!

Al-Shimr: What is with you, Suhail?

Do you fear to hear his name?

Or do you worry about me when hearing it?

It is me who killed him, Suhail.

I severed his head, myself, Suhail.

What do you fear for me?

A whole month and I still

See a body without a head,

Rising every night, touring the streets,

I see every night a great head dangling,

Crossing the roofs, sticking to doors and windows,

Looking for his shoulders, which I see closing together,

Until they almost meet,

The blood begins to flow about.

Then I see my sword and hand both smeared with blood.

So, what do you fear for me, Suhail? [He turns to Mālik]
I will quench your thirst, Mālik.
A whole month and you have been trying to find out.
I feel your eyes, your hands,
The quiver on your face,
I hear your panting running after details,
I know you are searching for a moment.
Mālik [Interrupting]: I am not.
Al-Shimr [Interrupting]: No excuses.
I, too, am trying to liberate myself, now,
From this moment.
A whole month I have kept it a secret, Mālik.
Of it I have what no one has.
Mālik: What, O Shimr?
Al-Shimr: Questions.
Mālik: Questions?
Al-Shimr: No one can ask except the one who severs another Ḥusain's head.
Mālik: What is the first question?
Al-Shimr: [He stares in Mālik's face, amazed, while the next question
Extends out, coming from all sides of the stage] Why? Why? Why? Why?
[The voice diminishes gradually]
Al-Shimr [Dazed]: Why? Why?
Malik: Why?
Al-Shimr: Every day I encourage myself and say:
If you must die now, Shimr,
You have to know in which prayer-direction you will die.
Then I catch this question:
And fix it before my eyes
Bring myself together, to face it,
To answer it.
But it branches out, Mālik, it grows leaves
And becomes thousands of questions.
[He kept a moment's silence, then continues]
I raised my sword to cut his throat,

He was thrown on the ground,
A large wound… I thought him dead.
Suddenly, he opened his eyes, Mālik!
I have never seen a protestation like his eyes!
For a moment, we were none but these:
A frightened killer, and the killed chasing him:
Merely two eyes.
Mālik: did he say anything?
Al-Shimr: Yes, one word: why?
You will not afraid as much as denouncing.
For a while, I thought all the swords in the world
Fail to sever his head…
I saw between his eyes a horrified, ravished man.
Mālik: Did you answer him?
Al-Shimr: Unconsciously, thus:
I said to him, because I hate you.
This assured serenity,
This look of prophetic eyes, I hate.
I said: you are a burden of purity
The land hates you, because you expose it
But my ordeal with you is much more than yours with me.
I am the one whose bad luck
Charged me with removing all chivalry from the earth.
[A moment's silence]
Mālik: then?
Al-Shimr: I turned my face away from his,
And, with both hands I pressed on the sword,
My fear was getting greater, greater
To become double the size of his pain,
I managed, and ended his pains,
Keeping my fear growing since then. [A moment's silence]
Then his head accompanied me,
With the eyes and voices of children,
The hair and voices of women
Crying and wailing…
I was alone, separate from the entire army

Carrying his head on my spear
And saw in the faces of the soldiers
That I'm something they fear, avoid.
Shall I tell you the truth, Mālik?
I felt the soldiers' hatred of me
Mālik: Your mere illusion.
Al-Shimr: No!
[Scene of the procession with Al-Ḥusain head,
Crying, lamentation, weeping, confusion]
One soldier: come here, Ḥudhaifa,
Why do you insert yourself where you do not belong?
Second soldier: I am contemplating Al- Ḥusain's face,
Which I have not seen before.
First soldier: Gloating, Ḥudhaifa?
Second soldier: No, by the creator of the world,
I feel he has an awe
Which makes the flesh go into the skin
From its greatness.
First soldier: Keep out then.
[He puts his hand on the second soldier's shoulder and walks away with him]
Ḥudhaifa, you are my brother,
I feel you may be home for the shadow of this head.
Leave the burden to those who severed it.
Let us go, and keep as far as you can
From Al-Shimr shadows. [Another scene of the same procession]
Soldier one: Hurry up… Hurry up.
Soldier two: Why the hurry?
Soldier one: To see how the caliph will meet Al-Shimr.
No doubt he would burden him with gold.
Soldier two: Not heavier than his burden now.
Soldier one: What?
Soldier two: [Redressing] I say what is that to us?
We lose if they lose
But when they win, their gains are for themselves.
Soldier one: I bet that Yazeed will load him with gold.

Al-Shimr: Yazeed has loaded me with gold.
Yazeed has loaded me with gold. [Side scene]
Al-Shimr voice: Fill my loads with silver or gold.
I have killed the protected lord.
The best when pedigree is told;
I killed the best man of parents bold.
Yazeed's voice: Are you competing, son of the lewd?
If you knew of him what you mentioned
How did you kill him?
Get out. If I see you again you will suffer my rancour.
[The scene diminishes]
Al-Shimr: [continues his hysterical laughter]
Yazeed loaded me with gold,
Yazeed loaded me with gold!
[His laughter turns to something like wailing]
Yazeed loaded me with poverty and crime,
He loaded me with poverty and crime
With poverty and crime!
Outcast like a scabby camel
Outcast, no one comes near me except who does not know me.
The gloating sympathiser
Outcast, outcast, outcast.
Suhail: [To Mālik, as Al-Shimr is under another fit,
Rising towards phantoms unseen by anyone]
I was afraid it would come to this,
But he stopped me when I tried…
Mālik: [interrupting]
You tried what, Suhail?
Do you fool yourself?
Command this wind to calm down now.
Who has the winds within him,
Do you control its reins?
Al-Shimr: Come and fill my loneliness
O eyes of those I waded in their blood
O the snoring of their throats
O shrieks of the widows

Disperse the gloom of silence around me
For I am lonesome, lonesome, lonesome.

ACT III

Time: The present. Place: Koofa, or any place where men may meet

Chorus: Water differs,
The faces and names differ,
But like the buckets of the waterwheel,
They look alike when they turn
They entangle when they turn.
Christ: [On the cross on the background of the stage]
Because I scattered my body,
Among the people,
Because I bore their suffering,
Because I used my own name.
Christ: [A crucified black man] Because I scattered my body among the people
Christ: [Hanged] Because I bore their suffering.
Christ: [Shot by bullets] Because I used my own name
[Voices from all sides of the stage]:
-- Because I scattered among…
-- Because I bore…
-- Because…
-- Because…
Chorus: Every Time carries its dead,
Every place buries its dead,
And the waterwheel turns.
-- Time begets times.
Death begets times
Death begets man
But fear begets flood

But fear begets flood. [The chorus disappears]
Ámmār: [Calling as he comes in to surprise everybody]
O people!
The clouds alighted in your land
The clouds alighted in your land
O people!
-- What, Ámmār? -- What, Ámmār?
Ámmār: A cloud, a cloud alighted in the entrance of your houses,
Asking, were you hit by thirst?
-- Be clear, Ámmār… Be clear.
Ámmār: O people of Koofa,
For a thousand years you bite your fingers in repentance,
For a thousand years your thirsty lifts the cup
To see a line of blood in the water,
For a thousand years…
You inscribe on your heads
On your backs, on your chests the histories of your forefathers,
Saying we wish, saying were we, saying had we…
Here he is now, if you were truthful.
-- Who is he, -- who?—Speak!
Ámmār: Al-Ḥusain's envoy.
[A group of people jump at him as the news causes a shock to all]
--Al-Ḥusain's envoy?
Ámmār: At the entrance of Koofa now. Anyone to pledge him allegiance
[They look at each other, tongue-tied, some steal away]
Ámmār: Al-Ḥusain's envoy has come to you. Anyone to pledge him allegiance?
Ḥārith :[Jumping at him] Easy, easy, what is this Ámmār?
Ámmār: What, Ḥārith?
Ḥārith: Is it a question you're asking?
Ámmār: But the news I am carrying.
Ḥārith: If you were a good news carrier, then you have not done well.

Ámmār: Have I not?
Ḥārith: No, by God. It is the lifetime joy
Which you almost turned into grief
By asking: who would pledge him allegiance?
As if you were pushing certainty into doubt.
[Others sneak away]
Ámmār [Looking at him and those pulling out]
Ḥārith: Has… doubt pulled away, O son of Abi-Awf?
[Pulling him aside] Woe, Ámmār! Have we not agreed yesterday to pledge?
Ámmār: We have.
Ḥārith: Why do you sound as if you are begging?
Ámmār: Woe! The matter and the man are greater than your insult.
Ḥārith: So, why?
Ámmār: You are the first who knows why, son of Abi-Awf.
[They look at each other for a long while]
Ḥārith [Addressing his audience]: O people of Kufa,
Have we not agreed on the pledge yesterday?
Ámmār: [As the whole audience hears him]
Will you still repeat your question, Ḥārith?
You know we have all agreed.
But you know we have not done that except secretly.
Ḥārith: And now we shall announce it,
And I will be the first to do so, Ámmār,
The first to do so.
Ámmār: [To himself] The first to do so, but you will hand him over,
Before the creek of the cock.
[He moves to stand on a high spot. Ma‹tooq interrupts]
Ma‹tooq: No, by God. None will start it but me.
Others: [Rising to them] But we shall start it.
Another: Easy, Ḥārith; easy Ma‹tooq. What is this?
Has the matter clouded so all men have lost where they stand?
[He turns to the group]
O people of Koofa,
This is Shamrān Al-Ḍāri. Does anyone not know him?

Make way for the aldermen of the two rivers.
No one but Shamrān should start the pledge.
Ámmār: [To himself, as Shamrān proceeds to the high spot]
Thus, always.
A thousand years and your voices are like this.
A thousand years and your bodies are like this.
All bare-footed compete until they lose hope,
To find a space among you that you did not step on
And in one moment
The one who seeks your succour finds himself naked
And your daggers race to kill him,
Before his enemies dare.
Shmrān: [Assuming the high spot]
Let him listen to me who cares,
Let him listen who cares!
Myself, my clan, and all my followers
Have promised allegiance to Al-Ḥusain
As a Caliph, O my people!
Myself, my clan and… [Others sneak out]
-- We also promise allegiance
-- These are our testimonies.
Fifty from Abdelazeez house.
[Two people withdraw to a corner on the stage]
The first: What is your opinion?
The second: What is that to us? It is their allegiance.
You have your head, Ḥamdān, escape with it,
Then bow it to whoever becomes caliph. Let's go. [They exit]
-- And twenty from Na‹mān's house
Ḥārith: Easy, easy!
-- Register twenty from Al-Anṣāri house.
-- A hundred from Shihābul-Deen house.
[Three wretched looking, barefooted persons, move
Separately from different sides of the stage]
The first: Can anyone hear me?
The second: Can anyone hear me?
The third: Can anyone hear me?
The three together: Can anyone hear us?

-- Two hundred men from Ḍiā'udeen house.
The three: Can anyone hear us? We are three people…
-- A hundred and thirty hands from Jalāl house;
Each hand is placed on the trigger.
The three: Who will write for us?
We are three people who have nothing but ourselves.
Rasheed: [Entering to face the group]
What is this? What are you doing, Ḥārith?
[A confusion flares among men present. Then dead silence]
Ḥārith: As you see. We are confirming the pledge to Al-Ḥusain.
Rasheed: What???
Ḥārith: I say we are here to pledge allegiance to Al-Ḥusain.
Before the day passes, we shall collect men and arms.
The three: Who would collect these names for us?
We are three people…
Rasheed: [Interrupting] Shut up. From which house are you?
The three: We have no house.
Rasheed: In whose name then?
The three: Our names.
Rasheed: Yours?
Ḥārith: Easy Rasheed!
Rasheed: You should calm down Ḥārith.
What are you going to do with these names?
Ḥārith: I said it is the pledge of allegiance, Rasheed.
Rasheed: Ḥārith, perhaps you have not forgotten
That Al-Ḥusain shall be killed within thirty days?
[Voices from the people present]: Will be killed within Thirty days?
Rasheed: And here you are collecting names of his followers.
Ḥārith: How dare you …?
Rasheed: [Interrupting] But tell them, O Ḥārith ibn Abi-ʿAwf
That you, before daybreak, will hand this prophet over
To his enemies, then he would be killed.
Voices: A plot, then.
Others: A planned plot [They all attack Ḥārith]
Give us back our names. Give us back our names.

Ámmār: [Trying to stop them from attacking Ḥārith]
O people… Do not let your enemies overpower you,
O folks…
The attackers: give us back our names.
-- Sa‹eed, Tear out the papers from his hands.
[They overpower Ḥārith and snatch the papers from him]
-- Give them back, give them back to us.
[They exit all. Ámmār, Ḥārith, Rasheed,
And the three barefooted ones remain on the scene].
Ámmār: May God disfigure your faces,
May God disfigure whoever seeks your help.
A thousand years and you lead your children to hope,
A thousand years and the baby grows on your women's laps
Hoping to wear a shroud
To fight for an honour, sold by its folks.
How can any of you enter his house?
[He turns to the three barefooted ones]
And you, the barefooted till doomsday,
You who come and go, and not a single bit
Of its grace is caught by your clothes.
For a thousand years I watch
To see if any of you asks about the way of safety,
But you come and go…
And your death leaves a sign on my forehead.
Let us go, you the best on this earth.

Rasheed: [Holding them] Where to, Ámmār? [They stop]

Do you think that you are escaping with them?

Their necks will be severed before they reach the market gate,

And you, at their top.

The three: Listen, you!

We know we shall die.

We pledged allegiance at Ṭaff and we died.

We pledged him in Sinai and died.

We pledged him at Tal-al- Za‹tar yesterday and died,

We pledge him in the occupied land every day,

And we die. [They turn to Ámmār]

Let us go, Al-Ḥusain follower.
[They exit. Ḥārith and Rasheed remain]
Rasheed: What has happened, Ḥārith?
For a thousand years we have been playing our roles,
You used to play your role to perfection,
So why did you intend to spoil the scene now?
Ḥārith: Listen Rasheed. Let us go back a thousand years.
Rasheed: [Surprised] Where to, Ḥārith?
Ḥārith: To the day this play began.
Rasheed: [Laughing] Just like that?
I was wondering to myself,
Why does Ḥārith alter his role?
You have forgotten, then…
[Continuing his laughter] no matter,
We go back to the first time it was played,
We shall define every detail in our roles.
Ḥārith: you will remain faithful to your role, Rasheed,
Until doomsday.
Rasheed: and you? Your role?
Are you not faithful to it?
Ḥārith: Forget my role now.
I have a painful talk about it with you…
I'm looking for something else.
[As if talking to himself] About a face,
I swear I know it,
As if I see a stamp on his face
But a thousand years have eroded my memory.
Rasheed: I do not care, Ḥārith, what you are looking for yourself.
But I want to be sure you do not miss my details,
No matter how small it may be in your role.
Ḥārith: Listen, you! What I look for myself
Is too large for you to realise…
As for my role, you have to know
That I shall change this role entirely.
Rasheed: What?!
Ḥārith: [Bursts in laughter] It is my turn to laugh now.

Rasheed: God take you! For a moment you were about to deceive me.

Ḥārith: How?

Rasheed: I thought you meant what you said

About your role…

You know how to clothe drollery with a face of seriousness.

Ḥārith: But now I clothe my seriousness

With a fearful face of drollery.

I shall refuse to send Al-Ḥusain's envoy to your soldiers

Rasheed: You?

Ḥārith: Yes.

Rasheed: [Laughing sarcastically]

For a thousand years you have been

Bringing him despite himself.

Ḥārith: I used to do that.

Rasheed: And you shall do now.

Ḥārith: Far from it… Listen Rasheed

How do you explain that I had given him up to you then?

Rasheed: [hesitating] Do you want the truth?

Ḥārith: Of course!

Rasheed: Your fear, Ḥārith!

I see nothing to explain your handing him over,

Except your fear.

Ḥārith: You are right.

Rasheed: And you shall hand him over once more, now.

Ḥārith: No!

Rasheed: Then we shall take him by force,

Then kill him before your eyes.

Ḥārith: Here we begin. This beginning I accept.

Rasheed, you know where this beginning will lead you to?

Ḥārith: What do you see?

Rasheed: All details remain as they happened,

Except one little point… Your own destiny…

Your own destiny is the only thing that will change…

You shall be killed, Ḥārith.

Ḥārith: [Bursts in laughter] I wish I shall be

[Continuing in laughter] I thought you were more intelligent.

Do you threaten me with death?

How can I reach it?!

That day, Rasheed,

When your soldiers besieged my house, a thousand years ago,

I was, from the beginning of the night,

Holding the balance of my situation to lift it:

You and your spurious life were in one scale,

Al-Ḥusain's envoy, with death, were in the other.

The hand of fear was shivering between you two,

When lifting the balance.

Do you know, Rasheed?

I have never despised myself like I did when death came…

I bore that remorse

I bore all my life my feeling of cowardice and betrayal

And like a blink of the eye, death came.

Why? Say why? In whose name, then?

Then you came and threatened me by death!

How I wish! How can I reach it?

What can you earn but bringing its time one hour earlier?

[A moment of silence]

Ḥārith: [Surprised] here he is!

Rasheed: Who?

Ḥārith: That face I was looking for, a thousand years ago.

[Scene: Yasir, his wife Aisha. Voices of Ubaidullah's soldiers.

Yasir's house, besieged by soldiers]

Aisha: What do you intend to do, Yasir?

Yasir: I do not know what to do, Um Sulaim!

Aisha: Silence is overwhelming.

They are now watching even the shadows in the roads of the town.

Entrances were closed,

Doors were closed,
And our house has no entrance to it,
Nor one out of it.
Every rock in the walls
Has a sword behind it, and eyes following it.

Rasheed [To Yāsir who is involved in a scene which he alone can see]:
I hope you could rethink, Ḥārith.
Ḥārith: [Interrupting bitterly] Silence, Rasheed.
I am now in the presence of the entire truth,
In the presence of the entire death.
So, grant me your silence, even for a minute.

[Rasheed keeps quiet, surprised, while the scene continues]
A voice from the soldiers outside the house:
Yāsir, your house is under surveillance.
Render us Ḥusain's followers,
And you and your children will be safe;
Or, woe to you, we are waiting for you until nightfall.
We are waiting for you until nightfall.
Aisha: [Surprised] Woe to me, Yāsir,
Sulaim is outside the door.
He has not returned since you sent him to Ámmār.
Yāsir: [Very concerned] Make sure, Aisha
He must be in some corner of the house.
Aisha: In some corner of the house?
You sent him to see Ámmār
How could he have returned without seeing you?
[She calls, as she is looking about the house]
Sulaim…Sulaim…
Yāsir [Calling as he is looking]
Sulaim…O Sulaim!
Sulaim: [From outside the house, held by the soldiers]
Leave me alone… Leave me alone…
Yāsir: That is Sulaim's voice. [Calling, horrified] Sulaim!
Sulaim: [Calling from outside]
Father, Ámmār sends you his greetings.

Ámmār is dead. Ámmār is dead. Ámmār is dead.
[Soldiers muffle his mouth]
Aisha: [Crying] Sulaim… My son… My darling!
[She tries to go out, but she is held by Yāsir]
Let me see my son; let me see him.
A voice from outside: O Yāsir, here is your son in our hands.
Open your door, or we slaughter him now.
Aisha: [Trying to release herself from her husband's hand]
No… No… We open the door… We open it.
Yasir: [Holding her tightly] Aisha, Aisha,
We are but two Muslims!
Remember, with something like this they tried Mohammad.
Aisha: [Trying to release herself from his hands] My only son!
Yāsir: Aisha, implore God's pardon. We are believers.
What do you secure for Sulaim
If you open this door now?
Aisha: His life is pawned to this door, Yāsir.
He lives if I open this door, Yāsir.
He lives if I open it… He lives…
Yāsir: He lives… No. But he escapes death.
To die a thousand times a day.
Do you know Aisha,
If you keep him now by this betrayal,
By violating this trust,
To which disgrace,
To which lifetime of shame you would hand him out?
He will be all his life: his step is cursed,
His forehead is cursed, laden with shame,
So he cannot lift his forehead for disgrace.
A voice from outside: O Yāsir,
Your son's neck is now under the sword,
If you do not open this door,
We should throw his head to you now.

Sulaim: [Crying from outside] Father!
Aisha: My son!
Yasir: Aisha. He will suffer for a moment,
A moment, then becomes silent.
Then his voice will survive until doomsday.
Aisha: My son!
Yāsir: Aisha, he is my son too. And because I love him so much
I'll save him be degraded and lowly.
If his life is pawned to your opening this door,
Then know that opening it is opening a door for him in Hell.
He will curse us every moment,
Because we did not protect God's trust in him,
That we have not protected the father's and mother's trust in him.
Aisha, it is God's wisdom,
So, anticipate God's reward for our loss.
Sulaim: [Crying under the sword…Yāsir is unconscious,
So his wife is released and she climbs to the roof of the house, crying]
Aisha: O my son! Oh my son!
Yāsir: [Tries to catch her, but he fails] Aisha, O Aisha!
Aisha: [Jumping out of the roof] Sulaim!
The followers of allegiance [Coming into the courtyard where Yāsir was]
-- What is this? What's going on, Yāsir?
Yāsir: [To himself, crying]
May God reward. May God reward, Sulaim!
May God reward and be my guardian, Um Sulaim!
-- What?
-- Did they kill your child, Yāsir?
-- And you did not tell us?
-- You leave us hiding away from the storm,
They slaughter your son, then kill his mother,
But you did not tell us?
-- What do you take us for?

-- Frightened ewes?
-- What shall I say now, Yāsir?
-- Implore God's mercy for us?
-- May God not pardon whoever remains alive
Among us now, Yāsir!
[To his friend]: Your swords, brothers of Al-Ḥusain.
Yāsir [Blocks their way, interrupting]
Easy, Aba-Umama, easy Aba-Suhail.
By God, my house will not turn you over,
As long as I live.
-- We go out together.
Yāsir: No, by the Lord!
Grant me the grace to beat the others
To my son and wife,
The grace of not seeing my charge killed before me…
Between us is the moment of passing through this door,
Then charge after me.
[The door opens, and he comes out drawing his sword]
Here I come Aisha… Here I come Sulaim…
[They follow him and the scene disappears]
Ḥārith: [Turns to Rasheed, as if awaking from a dream]
I was overlooking from my house roof;
I saw how you butchered his son,
And how his wife breathed her last,
And how you persecuted her.
I saw his gallantry in pushing you away
From his family. He was like a wounded lion,
His blood gushing all over. But he did not fall;
As if he was moving among you with a thousand swords.
Rasheed: Then, you were remembering now, Yāsir?
Ḥārith: I was recollecting now, Yāsir,
And compare between us.
Rasheed: But he died, and died all his followers.
Ḥārith: All of us died after that, Rasheed.
All of us died after that, Rasheed.
The difference is that I passed a thousand years,
To bypass my fear;

But Yāsir passed in a minute.
-- Once in my life I wept,
When I saw Yāsir falling;
I did not weep over him,
But like a widowed woman whimpering,
I was weeping for myself which I betrayed.
--Rasheed! Return to me that first moment,
So I can refuse to render that envoy,
Then here is my neck for you,
To server a thousand times, Rasheed,
Or, as many times as these years. But render me my head,
Then sever it, provided I reclaim the beginning
Rasheed: Do not hurry, Ḥārith.
It seems to me we shall see something unfamiliar,
Tonight. Go to meet your friend,
And wait for me with my men,
It is very difficult for me, as you have been my friend,
For a thousand years,
To sever your head, Ḥārith, with this sword of mine.
Ḥārith: That is all right, Rasheed,
One day you would be ashamed
To look at this sword of yours.
You would aspire even when the children
Look at you. Then our play will have another role.
Rasheed: You are dreaming, Ḥārith.
Ḥārith: But I can almost see that day…
How long it will take, I do not know.
But, like I can see you now, Rasheed,
In the same clarity and reality,
I can see them, all those who played parts
In this accursed play,
As they are revolting on the roles.
They will enter this same horrible stage,
But to change its scenes, one by one.
Then, it would be a beginning of an age
Which you do not know, now.
Rasheed: What I know is that you have left me no choice

About this head of yours. [They exit]

[Enter the Baptist, of the severed head, led by a guide]

The Baptist: What do you see, guide?

The guide: Crosses, as long as the eye can see.

Arms and legs turned dry on their woods;

Here is a boy who is kicking still.

The Baptist: Ask him. [The guide goes to the boy]

The guide: Who are you boy?

The boy: [A voice from behind the stage]:

The last believer, till now.

The last believer, till now.

The Baptist: Sometimes, my son I ask myself:

What use is it to look for your head, Yaḥya.

With the passing of every year,

I become more convinced

That if my head returns to my neck

I shall soon lose it.

The guide: Who will dare, Sir?

The Baptist: Time. Time is fast here, my son

In the past, everything used to come here slowly,

For death to arrive, needs time.

For fear to reach its height to become a killer,

Was in need for time, but…

Everything has changed now.

Joy comes and leaves in a blink of an eye.

Grief comes and leaves in a blink of an eye.

But fear… The moment it starts becomes a killer

So, my son, it seems useless to look for my head.

I know if it returns to my shoulders

How much fear it would raise.

The guide: Are you trying, Sir, to take us back without…

The Baptist [Interrupting]: No, we should continue searching,

Son, let us go. [They exit]

Al-Shimr: [Comes to this stage in modern clothes, addressing the audience]

O people of this time, who among you is Al-Ḥusain?

A young man in the audience: Who are you stranger?

Al-Shimr: [Surprised]: Who am I? Could you come closer!

The young man: Why?

Al-Shimr: Come closer to see my face clearly,

Perhaps you could recognise me.

The young man: [Gets out of the audience and goes up to the stage,

To look at Al-Shimr closely] I am still asking: who are you?

Al-Shimr: Now the question is adding to the matter a new dimension.

Has my face been cancelled that no one can recognise it anymore?

Or has it multiplied in your age so it can no longer

Look different from another face?

The young man: Don't you want to tell us now who you are?

Al-Shimr: What use is that? If your age cannot recognise me,

Then it is too late for me. And Al-Ḥusain is quite in control.

But if in your age I have multiplied,

So that faces are confused in your eyes,

Then it is too late for me too.

Another Shimr has now finished severing Al-Ḥusain's head.

Another young man from the audience: Then you are Shimr ibn Dhil-Jawshan!

Al-Shimr: Have I frightened you?

First young man: No, you can no longer frighten, Shimr.

This age cannot be frightened!

Al-Shimr: You are too grown-up to feel then…eh?

First young man: We grow up? Yes…Perhaps…

Al-Shimr: We meet in two days' time.

I hope we meet, and you are up to your claim.

Young man: You will see me, if you do not go far from your quarters.

Al-Shimr: Fear not. I promise I shall look for you.

Young man: The trouble of looking I should save you,
Ibn Dhil-Jawshan. You shall see me wherever you go.
[Threatening as he exits]

Al-Shimr: We shall see. We shall see.

Young man: [Calling] Shimr! O Shimr!

Al-Shimr: [Stops and turns to him]

Young man: If you really try to meet Al-Ḥusain,
To kill him, once more…

Al-Shimr: [Interrupting] To kill him for the thousandth time.

Young man: Listen then. I'll show you where to meet Al-Ḥusain:
Before you are all the palm-trees of Iraq,
And the Euphrates, which you remember.
Draw your sword, if you still have one,
And fall with it on all the palm tree necks.
If they are severed,
And all the palm tree heads rolled down
And the pollen spread all over the ground,
Smear it with blood like choral beads,
Then pass over to the Euphrates,
And order it to calm down its waves,
And to drop its neck, down to your sword.
-- If you cut off the Euphrates neck
And all the palm-tree heads,
O, Ibn Dhil-Jawshan,
Then you will have killed Al-Ḥusain in us.

Al-Shimr: Thus?!

Young man: Do not forget this…
All the palm-tree heads, O, Ibn Dhil-Jawshan;
One palm tree you miss,
And from it emerges Al-Ḥusain.

Al-Shimr: Thus?! What stops me now from severing this head of yours?

Young man: Do you see? Now you try to test your fear,
You are encouraging yourself to sever the head
Of a young palm-tree. Go on, O, Shimr
And make your fear the size of the entire earth,
Then come back. You shall find Al-Ḥusain waiting for you.
But you shall see him full of all Euphrates water,
Fenced by all these palm-trees.
Al-Shimr: [Exits] Woe on you!
[The young man exits from the stage. The Baptist and his guide enter]
The Baptist: What do you see, O, guide?
The guide: I see heaps of heads.
I see creatures which the souls avert.
Their necks are severed.
Their feet in pools of their blood planted,
Gathered around the hills of heads,
Each picks up a head, places it in his neck,
Then they march…
The Baptist: Where to?
The guide: Forward. There on the horizon
I see a banner raised, on a hillock,
And all are gathered around it.
The Baptist: Describe it to me.
The guide: At the top, there is a crescent.
Around wave dead bodies of men,
As if under it Bilāl called for prayers. (3)
The Baptist: What colour is it?
The guide: sable, like sand.
Red, like sand.
White, like sand.
The Baptist: Hurry up then!
The guide: Where to?
The Baptist: Pick up a head, and come back to me.
The guide: Master… Your head…
The Baptist: All this is my head. Hurry up before it is too late.

I realised it… I realised it…
You realised, Yaḥya, then, the beginning of the flood.
You realised, Yaḥya, then, the beginning of the flood.

Notes:

1. Koofa: second city built in the early years of Islam in 638, two years after Baṣra was built. It is situated on the banks of the Euphrates, and the four caliph Ali ibn Abi Ṭālib made it his capital. It was in that city that he was assassinated, and his shrine is visited by Shī ‘ite as a holy place.
2. Al-Ṭaff, the battle where Al-Ḥusain ibn Ali was skilled in an army led by the Umayyads, but the main army was formed by the people of Koofa.
3. Bilāl ibn Rabāḥ, an Abyssinian who was among the very first who embraced Islam. The Prophet chose him as his prayer-Caller.

*****